I0329674

C-2252 CAREER EXAMINATION SERIES

This is your PASSBOOK for...

Accounting Technician

Test Preparation Study Guide
Questions & Answers

NLC®
NATIONAL LEARNING CORPORATION®

212 Michael Drive, Syosset, NY 11791

(516) 921-8888 • www.passbooks.com

E-mail: info@passbooks.com

PUBLISHED IN THE UNITED STATES OF AMERICA

PASSBOOK® SERIES

THE *PASSBOOK® SERIES* has been created to prepare applicants and candidates for the ultimate academic battlefield – the examination room.

At some time in our lives, each and every one of us may be required to take an examination – for validation, matriculation, admission, qualification, registration, certification, or licensure.

Based on the assumption that every applicant or candidate has met the basic formal educational standards, has taken the required number of courses, and read the necessary texts, the *PASSBOOK® SERIES* furnishes the one special preparation which may assure passing with confidence, instead of failing with insecurity. Examination questions – together with answers – are furnished as the basic vehicle for study so that the mysteries of the examination and its compounding difficulties may be eliminated or diminished by a sure method.

This book is meant to help you pass your examination provided that you qualify and are serious in your objective.

The entire field is reviewed through the huge store of content information which is succinctly presented through a provocative and challenging approach – the question-and-answer method.

A climate of success is established by furnishing the correct answers at the end of each test.

You soon learn to recognize types of questions, forms of questions, and patterns of questioning. You may even begin to anticipate expected outcomes.

You perceive that many questions are repeated or adapted so that you can gain acute insights, which may enable you to score many sure points.

You learn how to confront new questions, or types of questions, and to attack them confidently and work out the correct answers.

You note objectives and emphases, and recognize pitfalls and dangers, so that you may make positive educational adjustments.

Moreover, you are kept fully informed in relation to new concepts, methods, practices, and directions in the field.

You discover that you are actually taking the examination all the time: you are preparing for the examination by "taking" an examination, not by reading extraneous and/or supererogatory textbooks.

In short, this PASSBOOK®, used directedly, should be an important factor in helping you to pass your test.

ACCOUNTING TECHNICIAN

DUTIES:
Under general supervision, performs a variety of specialized and complex clerical tasks in support of Commission's financial management programs inputting vendors' invoices; processing biweekly payroll transactions; processing weekly accounts payable vouchers; filing and maintaining check copies and backups accurately; setting up new vendors' files; checking and posting information on records or documents; reviewing and maintaining files and other records; operating office equipment; and performing other related duties as assigned.

SCOPE OF THE EXAMINATION:
Knowledge of and experience in automated accounting systems. Knowledge of federal and state general payroll requirements and applications. Ability to organize and maintain various files and reports; knowledge of data input/output equipment operation; performance of clerical functions such as filing and typing; basic financial and statistical analysis; ability to communicate effectively.

HOW TO PREPARE GUIDE FOR ACCOUNTING TECHNICIAN WRITTEN EXAMINATION

I. INTRODUCTION

The purpose of this booklet is to provide information about the written examination, which is used to place candidates on the Accounting Technician register. The register is used to hire candidates into Accounting Technician jobs.

II. EXAMINATION DESCRIPTION

The Accounting Technician examination consists of two parts – Part 1, Multiple-Choice Questions and Part 2, Workplace Situation Questions. Part 1 consists of a total of 71 multiple-choice questions and constitutes 50% of the total examination score. Part 2 consists of 36 workplace situation questions and constitutes the remaining 50% of the total examination score. You will have a total of three (3) hours to complete the entire examination.

Part 1: Multiple-Choice Questions

This part contains 71 multiple-choice questions designed to test your knowledge and abilities needed for performing the Accounting Technician work. It consists of six sections:

- **Section 1: Comparison and Contrast**. This section is designed to test your abilities to compare details (e.g., letters, numbers, words) quickly and accurately and detect differences, to focus on the task at hand, and/or to remember information such as words, numbers, pictures, and procedures.

- **Section 2: Knowledge of English**. This section of the examination consists of samples of written material containing errors in punctuation, grammar, and/o9r sentence structure. Punctuation errors may involve improper use or absence of commas, periods, quotation marks, question marks, colons, or semicolons. Grammatical errors may involve changes in tense, unclear pronoun references, incorrect sentence structure, and/or word(s) correctly spelled but inappropriately used.

- **Section 3: Mathematical Operations**. This section is designed to test your knowledge and ability to add, subtract, multiply, or divide whole numbers, percentages, and decimals and your ability to read and comprehend financial/numerical information and understand and analyze financial data.

- **Section 4: Reading Comprehension**. This section is designed to test your abilities to read and understand information and ideas presented in writing, to acquire knowledge by reading, thinking critically, and learning new material. It also tests your abilities to generate, organize, and analyze ideas logically, and to remember information such as words, numbers, pictures, and procedures.

- **Section 5: Computer Knowledge**. This section is designed to test your ability to use personal computers and software applications.

- **Section 6: Time Management**. This section is designed to test your ability to manage your own time and coordinate with others.

Each multiple-choice question has four answer choices. For each question, you should select the best choice from the four choices given. To respond to the question, you will need to use a No. 2 pencil to darken or fill in the bubble that corresponds to the answer of your choice on the answer sheet.

Part 2: Workplace Situation Questions

The second part of the examination contains situations that you may face on the job. Your task for this part of the examination is to review each workplace situation that is presented and to select the MOST effective response and the LEAST effective response to each situation from the four possible responses given.

III. SAMPLE EXAMINATION QUESTIONS AND ANSWERS

Sample Questions of Part 1 and Part 2 of the examination are provided below. Answers to these questions immediately follow. Please review these questions to familiarize yourself with the kinds of questions you will be asked and with the format of the examination. You should read each question carefully. It is easy to choose wrong answers simply by failing to pay attention to a part or parts of the question or by failing to read all answer choices.

Multiple-Choice Questions (Part 1)

Section 1. Comparison and Contrast

1. Your agency has purchased the following office supplies from Vendor A: one box of pens, nine reams of paper, three boxes of legal writing pads, and nine boxes of hanging folders. On the invoice, however, you notice that the vendor has billed you for one box of pens, three boxes of legal writing pads, nine boxes of manila folders, and nine reams of paper. Which item from the invoice is an error? 1.____
   A. One box of pens
   B. Nine boxes of manila folders
   C. Three boxes of legal writing pads
   D. None

Section 2. Knowledge of English

2. Which of the following sentences is correct? 2.____
   A. Three of my colleagues have published their papers in professional journals.

B. Three of my colleagues have published there papers in professional journals.
C. Three of my colleagues have published theirs papers in professional journals.
D. Three of my colleagues have published they're papers in professional journals.

Section 3. Mathematical Operations

3. You agreed to contribute one-eighth of your monthly income regularly to a charitable organization. Your average monthly income for the past two months was $1,232. How much was your contribution to the charitable organization for the past two months? 3.____
   A. $145 B. $154 C. $254 D. $308

Section 4. Reading Comprehension

4. Jean works for 20 hours this week on a part-time basis and earns $11 per hour. Carol also works on a part-time basis for 11 hours in the same week but earns $20 per hour. Based on this scenario, which of the following statements would be true? 4.____
   A. Carol's earnings for the week were more than Jean's.
   B. Carol's earnings for the week were less than Jean's.
   C. Carol's earnings for the week were twice as much as Jean's.
   D. Carol's earnings for the week were the same as Jean's.

Section 5. Computer Knowledge

5. To find out which version of a software application you are using, you would first click on the ______ command. 5.____
   A. View B. File C. Help D. Tools

Section 6. Time Management

6. Ed is unavailable from 2:00 P.M. to 3:30 P.M., Claudia from 9:00 A.M. to 12:00 P.M., and Lucy from 1:00 P M. to 3:00 P.M. When would be the best time for all three of them to meet for 1 hour and 30 minutes? 6.____
   A. 12:00 P.M. to 1:30 P.M. B. 12:30 P.M. to 2:00 P.M.
   C. 1:10 P.M. to 2:40 P.M. D. 3:30 P.M. to 5:00 P.M.

Workplace Situation Question (Part 2)

Read the situation below and identify the most effective response from among the four options. Then, identify the least effective response from the three remaining options.

A subordinate in your department has been tasked with finishing an important report for you, and the report is due to upper management early the next morning. This subordinate tells you that she has to leave work, but that she will return later that afternoon to finish the report. Later that evening, she has still not returned to work, and the report is still not completed. You would

A. go home, leaving her a note asking her to call you there
B. call her house and leave a message reminding her of the report
C. come in early the next morning to see if the report is done and take appropriate action
D. finish the report and meet with her the next morning to discuss the matter

7. What is the MOST effective response? 7.____

8. What is the LEAST effective response? 8.____

KEY (CORRECT ANSWERS)

1. Alternative B is the best answer because the office supplies your agency purchased from Vendor A include nine boxes of hanging folders rather than nine boxes of manila folders. Other items from the invoices listed as Alternatives A, C and D match those items ordered and, therefore, are correct.

2. Alternative A is the best answer because it is the only one with the correct use of the possessive pronoun "their." Alternatives B, C, and D contain incorrect use of words where "their" should have been used.

3. Alternative D is the best answer because, in order to determine the contributions for the past two months, you need to divide $1,232 by 8 for the first month, which equals $154, and then add another $154 as the contribution for the second month. The result is the contribution for the past two months, which totals $308.

4. Alternative D is the best answer because the total amount of Jean's earnings for the week (20 × $11 = $220) equals that of Carol's (11 × $20 = $220).

5. Alternative C is the best answer because information about the version of the software is on the Help drop-down menu, which can be accessed with a click on the Help command. None of the other commands listed in Alternatives A, B, and D contains this information.

6. Alternative D is the correct answer because the only time when all three people will be available for an hour and a half is between 3:30 P.M. and 5:00 P M. The times shown in the other alternatives represent conflicts in scheduling based on the information provided and, therefore, are incorrect choices.

7 Alternative D is the most effective response.

8. Alternative A is the least effective response.

IV. EXAMINATION ADMINISTRATION

If you meet minimum qualifications, you will receive a notification letter or postcard through the mail approximately two weeks before the scheduled test date. The notification letter or postcard provides information about the date, time, and location of the examination administration. On the day of the examination, you should plan to give yourself ample travel time so you can arrive at the examination site on time.

A. What to Bring to the Examination

You need to bring the following items to the testing site:

- **The notification letter or postcard** that you received from the State Personnel Department. You will **not be allowed** to take the examination without your notification letter or postcard.

- **A picture identification.** This could be a valid driver's license, a military identification card, a student identification card, or some form of picture identification. You need to have only one form of picture identification.

- **Several No. 2 pencils** with erasers. It is also recommended that you bring a highlighter pen.

- **A basic calculation** that allows you to perform simple arithmetic calculations such as addition, subtraction, division, and multiplication. You may bring a calculator to use for the Accounting Technician examination. Small solar powered or battery operated calculators that perform basic functions such as addition, subtraction, multiplication, division, square roots, or percentages are allowed. Calculators that plug in, utilize tape, have word processing, spelling, thesauruses, or other storage and retrieval capabilities (except basic memory functions) are not allowed. ***Calculators that are a feature on a cell phone are not permitted.*** Calculators are subject to inspection by exam monitors. Applicants may not borrow or share calculators at the exam site.

B. What Not to Bring to the Examination

You are not permitted to bring the following items to the testing site:

- This information booklet

- Any of your study materials, including notes, manuals, and other study materials.

- A cell phone or pager. Cell phones and pagers are allowed only if they are absolutely necessary. All cell phones and pagers must be set to the vibration or "silent" mode.

ACCOUNTING TECHNICIAN

SAMPLE QUESTIONS

Listed below are certain types of questions that will appear on the test. Work through the questions, and then check for the listed correct answer. There will be other types of questions on the test, so this is only a partial listing.

A. Each question consists of a series of numbers which progress in a definite order. Determine the pattern or trend in each sequence of numbers. Select the correct number, from the five alternatives, that would continue the series.

A. 5, ____, 15, 20, 25

A. 10
B. 11
C. 12
D. 13
E. 14

A (10) is the correct answer.

B. Compare each set or line of information in the LIST TO BE VERIFIED with the corresponding set in the CORRECT LIST. For each line in the LIST TO BE VERIFIED, indicate which of the following alternatives is true:

There is an error(s) in:

A. **One** column
B. **Two** columns
C. **Three** columns
D. **Four** columns
E. **None** of the columns

CORRECT LIST
June Ramplede
1833
253-05-0031
683-10

LIST TO BE VERIFIED

Name	Identifying Number	Resident City Code	Location Number
Jane Ramplede	1833	253-05-0031	683-10

The correct answer is A. There is an error in one column, the Name column.

C. Find the correct space in each listing for the name or code in italics on the first line of each question so that it will be in alphabetical and/or numerical order with the others.

02059625

A-
02059824
B-
02059913
C-
02064623
D-
02069102
E-

The correct answer is A.

D. 25.4 + 69.2 =

A. 84.6
B. 94.2
C. 94.6
D. 96.8
E. None of the above

C (94.6) is the correct answer.

E. Look at the numbers below. Circle the second number from the left. Add 3 to that number. What is the resulting answer?

2 5 7 1 4 7

A. 7
B. 8
C. 9
D. 10
E. 11

B (8) is the correct answer.

HOW TO TAKE A TEST

I. YOU MUST PASS AN EXAMINATION

A. WHAT EVERY CANDIDATE SHOULD KNOW

Examination applicants often ask us for help in preparing for the written test. What can I study in advance? What kinds of questions will be asked? How will the test be given? How will the papers be graded?

As an applicant for a civil service examination, you may be wondering about some of these things. Our purpose here is to suggest effective methods of advance study and to describe civil service examinations.

Your chances for success on this examination can be increased if you know how to prepare. Those "pre-examination jitters" can be reduced if you know what to expect. You can even experience an adventure in good citizenship if you know why civil service exams are given.

B. WHY ARE CIVIL SERVICE EXAMINATIONS GIVEN?

Civil service examinations are important to you in two ways. As a citizen, you want public jobs filled by employees who know how to do their work. As a job seeker, you want a fair chance to compete for that job on an equal footing with other candidates. The best-known means of accomplishing this two-fold goal is the competitive examination.

Exams are widely publicized throughout the nation. They may be administered for jobs in federal, state, city, municipal, town or village governments or agencies.

Any citizen may apply, with some limitations, such as the age or residence of applicants. Your experience and education may be reviewed to see whether you meet the requirements for the particular examination. When these requirements exist, they are reasonable and applied consistently to all applicants. Thus, a competitive examination may cause you some uneasiness now, but it is your privilege and safeguard.

C. HOW ARE CIVIL SERVICE EXAMS DEVELOPED?

Examinations are carefully written by trained technicians who are specialists in the field known as "psychological measurement," in consultation with recognized authorities in the field of work that the test will cover. These experts recommend the subject matter areas or skills to be tested; only those knowledges or skills important to your success on the job are included. The most reliable books and source materials available are used as references. Together, the experts and technicians judge the difficulty level of the questions.

Test technicians know how to phrase questions so that the problem is clearly stated. Their ethics do not permit "trick" or "catch" questions. Questions may have been tried out on sample groups, or subjected to statistical analysis, to determine their usefulness.

Written tests are often used in combination with performance tests, ratings of training and experience, and oral interviews. All of these measures combine to form the best-known means of finding the right person for the right job.

II. HOW TO PASS THE WRITTEN TEST

A. NATURE OF THE EXAMINATION

To prepare intelligently for civil service examinations, you should know how they differ from school examinations you have taken. In school you were assigned certain definite pages to read or subjects to cover. The examination questions were quite detailed and usually emphasized memory. Civil service exams, on the other hand, try to discover your present ability to perform the duties of a position, plus your potentiality to learn these duties. In other words, a civil service exam attempts to predict how successful you will be. Questions cover such a broad area that they cannot be as minute and detailed as school exam questions.

In the public service similar kinds of work, or positions, are grouped together in one "class." This process is known as *position-classification*. All the positions in a class are paid according to the salary range for that class. One class title covers all of these positions, and they are all tested by the same examination.

B. FOUR BASIC STEPS

1) Study the announcement

How, then, can you know what subjects to study? Our best answer is: "Learn as much as possible about the class of positions for which you've applied." The exam will test the knowledge, skills and abilities needed to do the work.

Your most valuable source of information about the position you want is the official exam announcement. This announcement lists the training and experience qualifications. Check these standards and apply only if you come reasonably close to meeting them.

The brief description of the position in the examination announcement offers some clues to the subjects which will be tested. Think about the job itself. Review the duties in your mind. Can you perform them, or are there some in which you are rusty? Fill in the blank spots in your preparation.

Many jurisdictions preview the written test in the exam announcement by including a section called "Knowledge and Abilities Required," "Scope of the Examination," or some similar heading. Here you will find out specifically what fields will be tested.

2) Review your own background

Once you learn in general what the position is all about, and what you need to know to do the work, ask yourself which subjects you already know fairly well and which need improvement. You may wonder whether to concentrate on improving your strong areas or on building some background in your fields of weakness. When the announcement has specified "some knowledge" or "considerable knowledge," or has used adjectives like "beginning principles of..." or "advanced ... methods," you can get a clue as to the number and difficulty of questions to be asked in any given field. More questions, and hence broader coverage, would be included for those subjects which are more important in the work. Now weigh your strengths and weaknesses against the job requirements and prepare accordingly.

3) Determine the level of the position

Another way to tell how intensively you should prepare is to understand the level of the job for which you are applying. Is it the entering level? In other words, is this the position in which beginners in a field of work are hired? Or is it an intermediate or advanced level? Sometimes this is indicated by such words as "Junior" or "Senior" in the class title. Other jurisdictions use Roman numerals to designate the level – Clerk I, Clerk II, for example. The word "Supervisor" sometimes appears in the title. If the level is not indicated by the title, check the description of duties. Will you be working under very close supervision, or will you have responsibility for independent decisions in this work?

4) Choose appropriate study materials

Now that you know the subjects to be examined and the relative amount of each subject to be covered, you can choose suitable study materials. For beginning level jobs, or even advanced ones, if you have a pronounced weakness in some aspect of your training, read a modern, standard textbook in that field. Be sure it is up to date and has general coverage. Such books are normally available at your library, and the librarian will be glad to help you locate one. For entry-level positions, questions of appropriate difficulty are chosen – neither highly advanced questions, nor those too simple. Such questions require careful thought but not advanced training.

If the position for which you are applying is technical or advanced, you will read more advanced, specialized material. If you are already familiar with the basic principles of your field, elementary textbooks would waste your time. Concentrate on advanced textbooks and technical periodicals. Think through the concepts and review difficult problems in your field.

These are all general sources. You can get more ideas on your own initiative, following these leads. For example, training manuals and publications of the government agency which employs workers in your field can be useful, particularly for technical and professional positions. A letter or visit to the government department involved may result in more specific study suggestions, and certainly will provide you with a more definite idea of the exact nature of the position you are seeking.

III. KINDS OF TESTS

Tests are used for purposes other than measuring knowledge and ability to perform specified duties. For some positions, it is equally important to test ability to make adjustments to new situations or to profit from training. In others, basic mental abilities not dependent on information are essential. Questions which test these things may not appear as pertinent to the duties of the position as those which test for knowledge and information. Yet they are often highly important parts of a fair examination. For very general questions, it is almost impossible to help you direct your study efforts. What we can do is to point out some of the more common of these general abilities needed in public service positions and describe some typical questions.

1) General information

Broad, general information has been found useful for predicting job success in some kinds of work. This is tested in a variety of ways, from vocabulary lists to questions about current events. Basic background in some field of work, such as sociology or economics, may be sampled in a group of questions. Often these are principles which have become familiar to most persons through exposure rather than through formal training. It is difficult to advise you how to study for these questions; being alert to the world around you is our best suggestion.

2) Verbal ability

An example of an ability needed in many positions is verbal or language ability. Verbal ability is, in brief, the ability to use and understand words. Vocabulary and grammar tests are typical measures of this ability. Reading comprehension or paragraph interpretation questions are common in many kinds of civil service tests. You are given a paragraph of written material and asked to find its central meaning.

3) Numerical ability

Number skills can be tested by the familiar arithmetic problem, by checking paired lists of numbers to see which are alike and which are different, or by interpreting charts and graphs. In the latter test, a graph may be printed in the test booklet which you are asked to use as the basis for answering questions.

4) Observation

A popular test for law-enforcement positions is the observation test. A picture is shown to you for several minutes, then taken away. Questions about the picture test your ability to observe both details and larger elements.

5) Following directions

In many positions in the public service, the employee must be able to carry out written instructions dependably and accurately. You may be given a chart with several columns, each column listing a variety of information. The questions require you to carry out directions involving the information given in the chart.

6) Skills and aptitudes

Performance tests effectively measure some manual skills and aptitudes. When the skill is one in which you are trained, such as typing or shorthand, you can practice. These tests are often very much like those given in business school or high school courses. For many of the other skills and aptitudes, however, no short-time preparation can be made. Skills and abilities natural to you or that you have developed throughout your lifetime are being tested.

Many of the general questions just described provide all the data needed to answer the questions and ask you to use your reasoning ability to find the answers. Your best preparation for these tests, as well as for tests of facts and ideas, is to be at your physical and mental best. You, no doubt, have your own methods of getting into an exam-taking mood and keeping "in shape." The next section lists some ideas on this subject.

IV. KINDS OF QUESTIONS

Only rarely is the "essay" question, which you answer in narrative form, used in civil service tests. Civil service tests are usually of the short-answer type. Full instructions for answering these questions will be given to you at the examination. But in case this is your first experience with short-answer questions and separate answer sheets, here is what you need to know:

1) Multiple-choice Questions

Most popular of the short-answer questions is the "multiple choice" or "best answer" question. It can be used, for example, to test for factual knowledge, ability to solve problems or judgment in meeting situations found at work.

A multiple-choice question is normally one of three types—

- It can begin with an incomplete statement followed by several possible endings. You are to find the one ending which *best* completes the statement, although some of the others may not be entirely wrong.
- It can also be a complete statement in the form of a question which is answered by choosing one of the statements listed.

- It can be in the form of a problem – again you select the best answer.

Here is an example of a multiple-choice question with a discussion which should give you some clues as to the method for choosing the right answer:

When an employee has a complaint about his assignment, the action which will *best* help him overcome his difficulty is to

A. discuss his difficulty with his coworkers
B. take the problem to the head of the organization
C. take the problem to the person who gave him the assignment
D. say nothing to anyone about his complaint

In answering this question, you should study each of the choices to find which is best. Consider choice "A" – Certainly an employee may discuss his complaint with fellow employees, but no change or improvement can result, and the complaint remains unresolved. Choice "B" is a poor choice since the head of the organization probably does not know what assignment you have been given, and taking your problem to him is known as "going over the head" of the supervisor. The supervisor, or person who made the assignment, is the person who can clarify it or correct any injustice. Choice "C" is, therefore, correct. To say nothing, as in choice "D," is unwise. Supervisors have and interest in knowing the problems employees are facing, and the employee is seeking a solution to his problem.

2) True/False Questions

The "true/false" or "right/wrong" form of question is sometimes used. Here a complete statement is given. Your job is to decide whether the statement is right or wrong.

SAMPLE: A roaming cell-phone call to a nearby city costs less than a non-roaming call to a distant city.

This statement is wrong, or false, since roaming calls are more expensive.

This is not a complete list of all possible question forms, although most of the others are variations of these common types. You will always get complete directions for answering questions. Be sure you understand *how* to mark your answers – ask questions until you do.

V. RECORDING YOUR ANSWERS

Computer terminals are used more and more today for many different kinds of exams.

For an examination with very few applicants, you may be told to record your answers in the test booklet itself. Separate answer sheets are much more common. If this separate answer sheet is to be scored by machine – and this is often the case – it is highly important that you mark your answers correctly in order to get credit.

An electronic scoring machine is often used in civil service offices because of the speed with which papers can be scored. Machine-scored answer sheets must be marked with a pencil, which will be given to you. This pencil has a high graphite content which responds to the electronic scoring machine. As a matter of fact, stray dots may register as answers, so do not let your pencil rest on the answer sheet while you are pondering the correct answer. Also, if your pencil lead breaks or is otherwise defective, ask for another.

Since the answer sheet will be dropped in a slot in the scoring machine, be careful not to bend the corners or get the paper crumpled.

The answer sheet normally has five vertical columns of numbers, with 30 numbers to a column. These numbers correspond to the question numbers in your test booklet. After each number, going across the page are four or five pairs of dotted lines. These short dotted lines have small letters or numbers above them. The first two pairs may also have a "T" or "F" above the letters. This indicates that the first two pairs only are to be used if the questions are of the true-false type. If the questions are multiple choice, disregard the "T" and "F" and pay attention only to the small letters or numbers.

Answer your questions in the manner of the sample that follows:

32. The largest city in the United States is
    A. Washington, D.C.
    B. New York City
    C. Chicago
    D. Detroit
    E. San Francisco

1) Choose the answer you think is best. (New York City is the largest, so "B" is correct.)
2) Find the row of dotted lines numbered the same as the question you are answering. (Find row number 32)
3) Find the pair of dotted lines corresponding to the answer. (Find the pair of lines under the mark "B.")
4) Make a solid black mark between the dotted lines.

VI. BEFORE THE TEST

Common sense will help you find procedures to follow to get ready for an examination. Too many of us, however, overlook these sensible measures. Indeed, nervousness and fatigue have been found to be the most serious reasons why applicants fail to do their best on civil service tests. Here is a list of reminders:

- Begin your preparation early – Don't wait until the last minute to go scurrying around for books and materials or to find out what the position is all about.
- Prepare continuously – An hour a night for a week is better than an all-night cram session. This has been definitely established. What is more, a night a week for a month will return better dividends than crowding your study into a shorter period of time.
- Locate the place of the exam – You have been sent a notice telling you when and where to report for the examination. If the location is in a different town or otherwise unfamiliar to you, it would be well to inquire the best route and learn something about the building.
- Relax the night before the test – Allow your mind to rest. Do not study at all that night. Plan some mild recreation or diversion; then go to bed early and get a good night's sleep.
- Get up early enough to make a leisurely trip to the place for the test – This way unforeseen events, traffic snarls, unfamiliar buildings, etc. will not upset you.
- Dress comfortably – A written test is not a fashion show. You will be known by number and not by name, so wear something comfortable.

- Leave excess paraphernalia at home – Shopping bags and odd bundles will get in your way. You need bring only the items mentioned in the official notice you received; usually everything you need is provided. Do not bring reference books to the exam. They will only confuse those last minutes and be taken away from you when in the test room.
- Arrive somewhat ahead of time – If because of transportation schedules you must get there very early, bring a newspaper or magazine to take your mind off yourself while waiting.
- Locate the examination room – When you have found the proper room, you will be directed to the seat or part of the room where you will sit. Sometimes you are given a sheet of instructions to read while you are waiting. Do not fill out any forms until you are told to do so; just read them and be prepared.
- Relax and prepare to listen to the instructions
- If you have any physical problem that may keep you from doing your best, be sure to tell the test administrator. If you are sick or in poor health, you really cannot do your best on the exam. You can come back and take the test some other time.

VII. AT THE TEST

The day of the test is here and you have the test booklet in your hand. The temptation to get going is very strong. Caution! There is more to success than knowing the right answers. You must know how to identify your papers and understand variations in the type of short-answer question used in this particular examination. Follow these suggestions for maximum results from your efforts:

1) Cooperate with the monitor

The test administrator has a duty to create a situation in which you can be as much at ease as possible. He will give instructions, tell you when to begin, check to see that you are marking your answer sheet correctly, and so on. He is not there to guard you, although he will see that your competitors do not take unfair advantage. He wants to help you do your best.

2) Listen to all instructions

Don't jump the gun! Wait until you understand all directions. In most civil service tests you get more time than you need to answer the questions. So don't be in a hurry. Read each word of instructions until you clearly understand the meaning. Study the examples, listen to all announcements and follow directions. Ask questions if you do not understand what to do.

3) Identify your papers

Civil service exams are usually identified by number only. You will be assigned a number; you must not put your name on your test papers. Be sure to copy your number correctly. Since more than one exam may be given, copy your exact examination title.

4) Plan your time

Unless you are told that a test is a "speed" or "rate of work" test, speed itself is usually not important. Time enough to answer all the questions will be provided, but this does not mean that you have all day. An overall time limit has been set. Divide the total time (in minutes) by the number of questions to determine the approximate time you have for each question.

5) Do not linger over difficult questions

If you come across a difficult question, mark it with a paper clip (useful to have along) and come back to it when you have been through the booklet. One caution if you do this – be sure to skip a number on your answer sheet as well. Check often to be sure that you have not lost your place and that you are marking in the row numbered the same as the question you are answering.

6) Read the questions

Be sure you know what the question asks! Many capable people are unsuccessful because they failed to *read* the questions correctly.

7) Answer all questions

Unless you have been instructed that a penalty will be deducted for incorrect answers, it is better to guess than to omit a question.

8) Speed tests

It is often better NOT to guess on speed tests. It has been found that on timed tests people are tempted to spend the last few seconds before time is called in marking answers at random – without even reading them – in the hope of picking up a few extra points. To discourage this practice, the instructions may warn you that your score will be "corrected" for guessing. That is, a penalty will be applied. The incorrect answers will be deducted from the correct ones, or some other penalty formula will be used.

9) Review your answers

If you finish before time is called, go back to the questions you guessed or omitted to give them further thought. Review other answers if you have time.

10) Return your test materials

If you are ready to leave before others have finished or time is called, take ALL your materials to the monitor and leave quietly. Never take any test material with you. The monitor can discover whose papers are not complete, and taking a test booklet may be grounds for disqualification.

VIII. EXAMINATION TECHNIQUES

1) Read the general instructions carefully. These are usually printed on the first page of the exam booklet. As a rule, these instructions refer to the timing of the examination; the fact that you should not start work until the signal and must stop work at a signal, etc. If there are any *special* instructions, such as a choice of questions to be answered, make sure that you note this instruction carefully.

2) When you are ready to start work on the examination, that is as soon as the signal has been given, read the instructions to each question booklet, underline any key words or phrases, such as *least, best, outline, describe* and the like. In this way you will tend to answer as requested rather than discover on reviewing your paper that you *listed without describing*, that you selected the *worst* choice rather than the *best* choice, etc.

3) If the examination is of the objective or multiple-choice type – that is, each question will also give a series of possible answers: A, B, C or D, and you are called upon to select the best answer and write the letter next to that answer on your answer paper – it is advisable to start answering each question in turn. There may be anywhere from 50 to 100 such questions in the three or four hours allotted and you can see how much time would be taken if you read through all the questions before beginning to answer any. Furthermore, if you come across a question or group of questions which you know would be difficult to answer, it would undoubtedly affect your handling of all the other questions.

4) If the examination is of the essay type and contains but a few questions, it is a moot point as to whether you should read all the questions before starting to answer any one. Of course, if you are given a choice – say five out of seven and the like – then it is essential to read all the questions so you can eliminate the two that are most difficult. If, however, you are asked to answer all the questions, there may be danger in trying to answer the easiest one first because you may find that you will spend too much time on it. The best technique is to answer the first question, then proceed to the second, etc.

5) Time your answers. Before the exam begins, write down the time it started, then add the time allowed for the examination and write down the time it must be completed, then divide the time available somewhat as follows:
   - If 3-1/2 hours are allowed, that would be 210 minutes. If you have 80 objective-type questions, that would be an average of 2-1/2 minutes per question. Allow yourself no more than 2 minutes per question, or a total of 160 minutes, which will permit about 50 minutes to review.
   - If for the time allotment of 210 minutes there are 7 essay questions to answer, that would average about 30 minutes a question. Give yourself only 25 minutes per question so that you have about 35 minutes to review.

6) The most important instruction is to *read each question* and make sure you know what is wanted. The second most important instruction is to *time yourself properly* so that you answer every question. The third most important instruction is to *answer every question.* Guess if you have to but include something for each question. Remember that you will receive no credit for a blank and will probably receive some credit if you write something in answer to an essay question. If you guess a letter – say "B" for a multiple-choice question – you may have guessed right. If you leave a blank as an answer to a multiple-choice question, the examiners may respect your feelings but it will not add a point to your score. Some exams may penalize you for wrong answers, so in such cases *only*, you may not want to guess unless you have some basis for your answer.

7) Suggestions
   a. Objective-type questions
      1. Examine the question booklet for proper sequence of pages and questions
      2. Read all instructions carefully
      3. Skip any question which seems too difficult; return to it after all other questions have been answered
      4. Apportion your time properly; do not spend too much time on any single question or group of questions

5. Note and underline key words – *all, most, fewest, least, best, worst, same, opposite,* etc.
6. Pay particular attention to negatives
7. Note unusual option, e.g., unduly long, short, complex, different or similar in content to the body of the question
8. Observe the use of "hedging" words – *probably, may, most likely,* etc.
9. Make sure that your answer is put next to the same number as the question
10. Do not second-guess unless you have good reason to believe the second answer is definitely more correct
11. Cross out original answer if you decide another answer is more accurate; do not erase until you are ready to hand your paper in
12. Answer all questions; guess unless instructed otherwise
13. Leave time for review

b. Essay questions
1. Read each question carefully
2. Determine exactly what is wanted. Underline key words or phrases.
3. Decide on outline or paragraph answer
4. Include many different points and elements unless asked to develop any one or two points or elements
5. Show impartiality by giving pros and cons unless directed to select one side only
6. Make and write down any assumptions you find necessary to answer the questions
7. Watch your English, grammar, punctuation and choice of words
8. Time your answers; don't crowd material

8) Answering the essay question

Most essay questions can be answered by framing the specific response around several key words or ideas. Here are a few such key words or ideas:

M's: manpower, materials, methods, money, management
P's: purpose, program, policy, plan, procedure, practice, problems, pitfalls, personnel, public relations

a. Six basic steps in handling problems:
1. Preliminary plan and background development
2. Collect information, data and facts
3. Analyze and interpret information, data and facts
4. Analyze and develop solutions as well as make recommendations
5. Prepare report and sell recommendations
6. Install recommendations and follow up effectiveness

b. Pitfalls to avoid
1. *Taking things for granted* – A statement of the situation does not necessarily imply that each of the elements is necessarily true; for example, a complaint may be invalid and biased so that all that can be taken for granted is that a complaint has been registered

2. *Considering only one side of a situation* – Wherever possible, indicate several alternatives and then point out the reasons you selected the best one
3. *Failing to indicate follow up* – Whenever your answer indicates action on your part, make certain that you will take proper follow-up action to see how successful your recommendations, procedures or actions turn out to be
4. *Taking too long in answering any single question* – Remember to time your answers properly

IX. AFTER THE TEST

Scoring procedures differ in detail among civil service jurisdictions although the general principles are the same. Whether the papers are hand-scored or graded by machine we have described, they are nearly always graded by number. That is, the person who marks the paper knows only the number – never the name – of the applicant. Not until all the papers have been graded will they be matched with names. If other tests, such as training and experience or oral interview ratings have been given, scores will be combined. Different parts of the examination usually have different weights. For example, the written test might count 60 percent of the final grade, and a rating of training and experience 40 percent. In many jurisdictions, veterans will have a certain number of points added to their grades.

After the final grade has been determined, the names are placed in grade order and an eligible list is established. There are various methods for resolving ties between those who get the same final grade – probably the most common is to place first the name of the person whose application was received first. Job offers are made from the eligible list in the order the names appear on it. You will be notified of your grade and your rank as soon as all these computations have been made. This will be done as rapidly as possible.

People who are found to meet the requirements in the announcement are called "eligibles." Their names are put on a list of eligible candidates. An eligible's chances of getting a job depend on how high he stands on this list and how fast agencies are filling jobs from the list.

When a job is to be filled from a list of eligibles, the agency asks for the names of people on the list of eligibles for that job. When the civil service commission receives this request, it sends to the agency the names of the three people highest on this list. Or, if the job to be filled has specialized requirements, the office sends the agency the names of the top three persons who meet these requirements from the general list.

The appointing officer makes a choice from among the three people whose names were sent to him. If the selected person accepts the appointment, the names of the others are put back on the list to be considered for future openings.

That is the rule in hiring from all kinds of eligible lists, whether they are for typist, carpenter, chemist, or something else. For every vacancy, the appointing officer has his choice of any one of the top three eligibles on the list. This explains why the person whose name is on top of the list sometimes does not get an appointment when some of the persons lower on the list do. If the appointing officer chooses the second or third eligible, the No. 1 eligible does not get a job at once, but stays on the list until he is appointed or the list is terminated.

X. HOW TO PASS THE INTERVIEW TEST

The examination for which you applied requires an oral interview test. You have already taken the written test and you are now being called for the interview test – the final part of the formal examination.

You may think that it is not possible to prepare for an interview test and that there are no procedures to follow during an interview. Our purpose is to point out some things you can do in advance that will help you and some good rules to follow and pitfalls to avoid while you are being interviewed.

What is an interview supposed to test?

The written examination is designed to test the technical knowledge and competence of the candidate; the oral is designed to evaluate intangible qualities, not readily measured otherwise, and to establish a list showing the relative fitness of each candidate – as measured against his competitors – for the position sought. Scoring is not on the basis of "right" and "wrong," but on a sliding scale of values ranging from "not passable" to "outstanding." As a matter of fact, it is possible to achieve a relatively low score without a single "incorrect" answer because of evident weakness in the qualities being measured.

Occasionally, an examination may consist entirely of an oral test – either an individual or a group oral. In such cases, information is sought concerning the technical knowledges and abilities of the candidate, since there has been no written examination for this purpose. More commonly, however, an oral test is used to supplement a written examination.

Who conducts interviews?

The composition of oral boards varies among different jurisdictions. In nearly all, a representative of the personnel department serves as chairman. One of the members of the board may be a representative of the department in which the candidate would work. In some cases, "outside experts" are used, and, frequently, a businessman or some other representative of the general public is asked to serve. Labor and management or other special groups may be represented. The aim is to secure the services of experts in the appropriate field.

However the board is composed, it is a good idea (and not at all improper or unethical) to ascertain in advance of the interview who the members are and what groups they represent. When you are introduced to them, you will have some idea of their backgrounds and interests, and at least you will not stutter and stammer over their names.

What should be done before the interview?

While knowledge about the board members is useful and takes some of the surprise element out of the interview, there is other preparation which is more substantive. It *is* possible to prepare for an oral interview – in several ways:

1) Keep a copy of your application and review it carefully before the interview

This may be the only document before the oral board, and the starting point of the interview. Know what education and experience you have listed there, and the sequence and dates of all of it. Sometimes the board will ask you to review the highlights of your experience for them; you should not have to hem and haw doing it.

2) Study the class specification and the examination announcement

Usually, the oral board has one or both of these to guide them. The qualities, characteristics or knowledges required by the position sought are stated in these documents. They offer valuable clues as to the nature of the oral interview. For example, if the job involves supervisory responsibilities, the announcement will usually indicate that knowledge of modern supervisory methods and the qualifications of the candidate as a supervisor will be tested. If so, you can expect such questions, frequently in the form of a hypothetical situation which you are expected to solve. NEVER go into an oral without knowledge of the duties and responsibilities of the job you seek.

3) Think through each qualification required

Try to visualize the kind of questions you would ask if you were a board member. How well could you answer them? Try especially to appraise your own knowledge and background in each area, *measured against the job sought*, and identify any areas in which you are weak. Be critical and realistic – do not flatter yourself.

4) Do some general reading in areas in which you feel you may be weak

For example, if the job involves supervision and your past experience has NOT, some general reading in supervisory methods and practices, particularly in the field of human relations, might be useful. Do NOT study agency procedures or detailed manuals. The oral board will be testing your understanding and capacity, not your memory.

5) Get a good night's sleep and watch your general health and mental attitude

You will want a clear head at the interview. Take care of a cold or any other minor ailment, and of course, no hangovers.

What should be done on the day of the interview?

Now comes the day of the interview itself. Give yourself plenty of time to get there. Plan to arrive somewhat ahead of the scheduled time, particularly if your appointment is in the fore part of the day. If a previous candidate fails to appear, the board might be ready for you a bit early. By early afternoon an oral board is almost invariably behind schedule if there are many candidates, and you may have to wait. Take along a book or magazine to read, or your application to review, but leave any extraneous material in the waiting room when you go in for your interview. In any event, relax and compose yourself.

The matter of dress is important. The board is forming impressions about you – from your experience, your manners, your attitude, and your appearance. Give your personal appearance careful attention. Dress your best, but not your flashiest. Choose conservative, appropriate clothing, and be sure it is immaculate. This is a business interview, and your appearance should indicate that you regard it as such. Besides, being well groomed and properly dressed will help boost your confidence.

Sooner or later, someone will call your name and escort you into the interview room. *This is it.* From here on you are on your own. It is too late for any more preparation. But remember, you asked for this opportunity to prove your fitness, and you are here because your request was granted.

What happens when you go in?

The usual sequence of events will be as follows: The clerk (who is often the board stenographer) will introduce you to the chairman of the oral board, who will introduce you to the other members of the board. Acknowledge the introductions before you sit down. Do not be surprised if you find a microphone facing you or a stenotypist sitting by. Oral interviews are usually recorded in the event of an appeal or other review.

Usually the chairman of the board will open the interview by reviewing the highlights of your education and work experience from your application – primarily for the benefit of the other members of the board, as well as to get the material into the record. Do not interrupt or comment unless there is an error or significant misinterpretation; if that is the case, do not hesitate. But do not quibble about insignificant matters. Also, he will usually ask you some question about your education, experience or your present job – partly to get you to start talking and to establish the interviewing "rapport." He may start the actual questioning, or turn it over to one of the other members. Frequently, each member undertakes the questioning on a particular area, one in which he is perhaps most competent, so you can expect each member to participate in the examination. Because time is limited, you may also expect some rather abrupt switches in the direction the questioning takes, so do not be upset by it. Normally, a board member will not pursue a single line of questioning unless he discovers a particular strength or weakness.

After each member has participated, the chairman will usually ask whether any member has any further questions, then will ask you if you have anything you wish to add. Unless you are expecting this question, it may floor you. Worse, it may start you off on an extended, extemporaneous speech. The board is not usually seeking more information. The question is principally to offer you a last opportunity to present further qualifications or to indicate that you have nothing to add. So, if you feel that a significant qualification or characteristic has been overlooked, it is proper to point it out in a sentence or so. Do not compliment the board on the thoroughness of their examination – they have been sketchy, and you know it. If you wish, merely say, "No thank you, I have nothing further to add." This is a point where you can "talk yourself out" of a good impression or fail to present an important bit of information. Remember, *you close the interview yourself.*

The chairman will then say, "That is all, Mr. ______, thank you." Do not be startled; the interview is over, and quicker than you think. Thank him, gather your belongings and take your leave. Save your sigh of relief for the other side of the door.

How to put your best foot forward

Throughout this entire process, you may feel that the board individually and collectively is trying to pierce your defenses, seek out your hidden weaknesses and embarrass and confuse you. Actually, this is not true. They are obliged to make an appraisal of your qualifications for the job you are seeking, and they want to see you in your best light. Remember, they must interview all candidates and a non-cooperative candidate may become a failure in spite of their best efforts to bring out his qualifications. Here are 15 suggestions that will help you:

1) Be natural – Keep your attitude confident, not cocky

If you are not confident that you can do the job, do not expect the board to be. Do not apologize for your weaknesses, try to bring out your strong points. The board is interested in a positive, not negative, presentation. Cockiness will antagonize any board member and make him wonder if you are covering up a weakness by a false show of strength.

2) Get comfortable, but don't lounge or sprawl

Sit erectly but not stiffly. A careless posture may lead the board to conclude that you are careless in other things, or at least that you are not impressed by the importance of the occasion. Either conclusion is natural, even if incorrect. Do not fuss with your clothing, a pencil or an ashtray. Your hands may occasionally be useful to emphasize a point; do not let them become a point of distraction.

3) Do not wisecrack or make small talk

This is a serious situation, and your attitude should show that you consider it as such. Further, the time of the board is limited – they do not want to waste it, and neither should you.

4) Do not exaggerate your experience or abilities

In the first place, from information in the application or other interviews and sources, the board may know more about you than you think. Secondly, you probably will not get away with it. An experienced board is rather adept at spotting such a situation, so do not take the chance.

5) If you know a board member, do not make a point of it, yet do not hide it

Certainly you are not fooling him, and probably not the other members of the board. Do not try to take advantage of your acquaintanceship – it will probably do you little good.

6) Do not dominate the interview

Let the board do that. They will give you the clues – do not assume that you have to do all the talking. Realize that the board has a number of questions to ask you, and do not try to take up all the interview time by showing off your extensive knowledge of the answer to the first one.

7) Be attentive

You only have 20 minutes or so, and you should keep your attention at its sharpest throughout. When a member is addressing a problem or question to you, give him your undivided attention. Address your reply principally to him, but do not exclude the other board members.

8) Do not interrupt

A board member may be stating a problem for you to analyze. He will ask you a question when the time comes. Let him state the problem, and wait for the question.

9) Make sure you understand the question

Do not try to answer until you are sure what the question is. If it is not clear, restate it in your own words or ask the board member to clarify it for you. However, do not haggle about minor elements.

10) Reply promptly but not hastily

A common entry on oral board rating sheets is "candidate responded readily," or "candidate hesitated in replies." Respond as promptly and quickly as you can, but do not jump to a hasty, ill-considered answer.

11) Do not be peremptory in your answers

A brief answer is proper – but do not fire your answer back. That is a losing game from your point of view. The board member can probably ask questions much faster than you can answer them.

12) Do not try to create the answer you think the board member wants

He is interested in what kind of mind you have and how it works – not in playing games. Furthermore, he can usually spot this practice and will actually grade you down on it.

13) Do not switch sides in your reply merely to agree with a board member

Frequently, a member will take a contrary position merely to draw you out and to see if you are willing and able to defend your point of view. Do not start a debate, yet do not surrender a good position. If a position is worth taking, it is worth defending.

14) Do not be afraid to admit an error in judgment if you are shown to be wrong

The board knows that you are forced to reply without any opportunity for careful consideration. Your answer may be demonstrably wrong. If so, admit it and get on with the interview.

15) Do not dwell at length on your present job

The opening question may relate to your present assignment. Answer the question but do not go into an extended discussion. You are being examined for a *new* job, not your present one. As a matter of fact, try to phrase ALL your answers in terms of the job for which you are being examined.

Basis of Rating

Probably you will forget most of these "do's" and "don'ts" when you walk into the oral interview room. Even remembering them all will not ensure you a passing grade. Perhaps you did not have the qualifications in the first place. But remembering them will help you to put your best foot forward, without treading on the toes of the board members.

Rumor and popular opinion to the contrary notwithstanding, an oral board wants you to make the best appearance possible. They know you are under pressure – but they also want to see how you respond to it as a guide to what your reaction would be under the pressures of the job you seek. They will be influenced by the degree of poise you display, the personal traits you show and the manner in which you respond.

ABOUT THIS BOOK

This book contains tests divided into Examination Sections. Go through each test, answering every question in the margin. We have also attached a sample answer sheet at the back of the book that can be removed and used. At the end of each test look at the answer key and check your answers. On the ones you got wrong, look at the right answer choice and learn. Do not fill in the answers first. Do not memorize the questions and answers, but understand the answer and principles involved. On your test, the questions will likely be different from the samples. Questions are changed and new ones added. If you understand these past questions you should have success with any changes that arise. Tests may consist of several types of questions. We have additional books on each subject should more study be advisable or necessary for you. Finally, the more you study, the better prepared you will be. This book is intended to be the last thing you study before you walk into the examination room. Prior study of relevant texts is also recommended. NLC publishes some of these in our Fundamental Series. Knowledge and good sense are important factors in passing your exam. Good luck also helps. So now study this Passbook, absorb the material contained within and take that knowledge into the examination. Then do your best to pass that exam.

EXAMINATION SECTION

EXAMINATION SECTION
TEST 1

DIRECTIONS: Each question or incomplete statement is followed by several suggested answers or completions. Select the one that BEST answers the question or completes the statement. *PRINT THE LETTER OF THE CORRECT ANSWER IN THE SPACE AT THE RIGHT.*

Questions 1-7.

DIRECTIONS: Questions 1 through 7 are to be answered on the basis of the following income statement.

Laura Lee's Bridal Shop
Income Statement
For the Year Ended December 31, 2018

Revenue:		
New & Used Bridal Gowns & Accessories		$55,000
Expenses:		
Advertisement Expense	$ 2,000	
Salaries Expense	12,000	
Dry cleaning & Alterations	10,000	
Utilities	1,500	
Total Expenses		25,500
Net Income		$29,500

1. What is the period of time covered by this income statement? 1.____

A. January-December 2017
B. December 2018
C. January 2017-December 2018
D. January-December 2018

2. What is the source of the revenue? 2.____

A. New and used bridal gowns, advertisements, salaries, dry cleaning, and utilities
B. Advertisements, salaries, dry cleaning, alterations, and utilities
C. New and used bridal gowns and accessories
D. Net income

3. What is the total revenue? 3.____

A. $25,500 B. $55,000 C. $29,500 D. $79,500

4. Which of the following are expenses? 4.____

A. Salaries
B. New and used bridal gowns and accessories
C. Revenue
D. New and used bridal gowns, advertisements, and dry cleaning

5. What are the total expenses? 5.____

A. $55,000 B. $29,500 C. $79,500 D. $25,500

6. There is a resulting net income because 6.____

   A. total revenue and total expenses are combined
   B. net income is greater than total revenue
   C. the total revenue is greater than total expenses
   D. the total revenue is less than total expenses

7. Is this statement an interim statement? 7.____

   A. *Yes*, because it covers an entire accounting period
   B. *No*, because it covers an entire accounting period
   C. *Yes*, because it covers a period of less than a year
   D. *No*, because it covers a period of more than a year

8. What is the name of the accounting report that may show either a net profit or a net loss for an accounting period? 8.____

   A. Income statement
   B. Balance sheet
   C. Statement of capital
   D. Classified balance sheet

9. What are the two main parts of the body of the income statement? 9.____

   A. Cash and Capital
   B. Revenue and Expenses
   C. Liabilities and Capital
   D. Assets and Notes Payable

10. If total revenue exceeds total expenses for an accounting period, what is the difference called? 10.____

    A. Gross income
    B. Total liabilities
    C. Total assets
    D. Net income

11. In the body of a balance sheet, what are the three sections called? 11.____

    A. Assets and liabilities
    B. Cash, liabilities, and revenue
    C. Assets, liabilities, and capital
    D. Revenue, assets, and capital

12. What business record shows the results of the proprietor's borrowing assets from the business, usually in anticipation of profits? 12.____

    A. Proprietor's withdrawals
    B. Accounts payable
    C. Liabilities and Capital
    D. Total liabilities

Questions 13-24.

DIRECTIONS: For each transaction given for Mona's Magic Moments Hair Salon in Questions 13 through 24, identify which journal the transaction should be recorded in.

13. April 1: Mona, the owner, paid the month's rent - $600.00; check no. 356. 13.____

    A. General
    B. Cash disbursements
    C. Purchases
    D. Sales

14. April 6: the salon purchased $300.00 worth of styling products on account from Pomme de Terre Company. 14.____

A. Cash disbursements B. General
C. Sales D. Purchases

15. April 8: sold $100.00 worth of hair products on account to Mrs. Angela Bray. 15.____

A. Sales B. Purchases
C. Cash disbursements D. General

16. April 11: the owner, Mona Ramen, withdrew $80.00 of styling products for personal use. 16.____

A. Sales B. Cash receipts
C. General D. Cash disbursements

17. April 13: paid Pomme de Terre Company $300.00 on account; check 357. 17.____

A. Purchases B. Cash disbursements
C. Cash receipts D. General

18. April 15: cash sales to date were $4,607.00. 18.____

A. Cash disbursements B. Purchases
C. Sales D. General

19. April 17: issued credit slip #17 to Mrs. Angela Bray for $25.00 for merchandise returned. 19.____

A. Cash disbursements B. Cash receipts
C. Sales D. General

20. April 19: paid electric bill for $250.00; check no. 358. 20.____

A. Cash disbursements B. Purchases
C. General D. Cash receipts

21. April 21: received $75.00 from Mrs. Angela Bray for balance due on account. 21.____

A. Sales B. Cash disbursements
C. Cash receipts D. Purchases

22. April 23: sold $88.00 of hair products on account to Ms. Tania Alioto. 22.____

A. Purchases B. Sales
C. Cash disbursements D. Cash receipts

23. April 27: purchased $500.00 of equipment from Salon Stylings Merchandisers on account. 23.____

A. Cash disbursements B. Sales
C. General D. Purchases

24. April 30: cash sales to date were $5023.00. 24.____

A. Purchases B. Sales
C. Cash receipts D. General

Questions 25-30.

DIRECTIONS: Questions 25 through 30 are to be answered on the basis of the following ledger for a barbecue take-out restaurant owned and operated by Ruby Joiner.

Cash	
450	150
212	125
328	440
172	125
250	70
275	150
325	50

Accounts Receivable	
360	170
250	100
165	120
100	60

Delivery Equipment	
5,000	
4,000	
3,000	

Supplies	
40	
65	
30	
25	

Ruby Joiner, Capital	
	8,200
	2,000
	2,097

Accounts Payable	
10	600
15	300
	200

Ruby Joiner, Drawing	
225	
175	
200	

Advertising Expense	
40	
45	

Delivery Income	
	400
	350
	250
	100

Trucking Expense	
100	
50	

Telephone Expense	
80	
40	
20	

25. What is the balance on the Cash account shown above? 25.____

A. 2,012.00 B. 1,110.00 C. 3,122.00 D. 902.00

26. What is the balance on the Accounts receivable account shown above? 26.____

A. 425.00 B. 875.00 C. 450.00 D. 1315.00

27. What is the balance on the Accounts payable account shown above? 27.____

A. 1100.00 B. 1075.00 C. 25.00 D. 1125.00

28. Which of the above accounts has a balance of 1100.00? 28.____

A. Accounts payable
B. Delivery Income
C. Cash
D. Delivery equipment

29. Which of the above accounts has a balance of 12,000.00? 29.____

A. Ruby Joiner, Capital
B. Cash and Accounts receivable combined
C. Delivery equipment
D. None of the accounts

30. If you made a balance sheet out of the information listed above, Ruby Joiner's total assets would be 30.____

A. 14,472.00 B. 12,297.00 C. 13,392.00 D. 13,487.00

Questions 31-34.

DIRECTIONS: Questions 31 through 34 are to be answered on the basis of the following information, to be included on a checking deposit ticket.

Five $20 bills; 11 $10 bills; 6 $5 bills; 47 $1 bills; 200 half dollars; 120 quarters; 112 dimes; 320 nickels; 67 pennies. Second National Bank (73-124) check of 152.34; Bank of the Midwest (13-298) check of 68.37; Great National Bank (32-165) check of 185.06.

31. What is the TOTAL currency for this deposit? 31.____

A. $387 B. $287 C. $444.87 D. $157.87

32. What is the TOTAL coin for this deposit? 32.____

A. $387 B. $287 C. $444.87 D. $157.87

33. What is the check total for this deposit? 33.____

A. $692.77 B. $406 C. $405.77 D. $850.64

34. What is the TOTAL deposit? 34.____

A. $444.87 B. $692.77 C. $851 D. $850.64

Questions 35-37.

DIRECTIONS: Questions 35 through 37 are to be answered on the basis of the following petty cash journal.

Date	Receipt No.	To Whom Paid	For What	Acct.#	Amount
10/2	1	Anna Jones - Mail	Postage	548	13.50
10/2	2	Jim Collins	Messenger	525	5.75
10/4	3	Anna Jones - Mail	Postage	548	13.50
10/5	4	Lucky Stores	Coffee	515	7.34
10/6	5	Tom Allen	Lunch w/customer	525	11.38

35. What is the TOTAL disbursement from this fund for the time period 10/1 through 10/6? 35.____

A. $51.47 B. $40.09 C. $61.47 D. $26.59

36. How much money was disbursed to Account #548 during the time period 10/1-10/16? 36.____

A. $51.47 B. $26 C. $27 D. $34.34

37. If the fund began the month with a total of $100.00, what amount was left in the fund at the end of business on 10/5? 37.____

A. $48.53 B. $59.91 C. $51.47 D. $40.09

Questions 38-40.

DIRECTIONS: Questions 38 through 40 are to be answered on the basis of the following information.

A promissory note dated December 1, 2018, bearing interest at a rate of 12% and due in 90 days, is sent to a creditor. The face value of the note is $900.

38. What is the due date of the promissory note? 38.____

A. January 15, 2019 B. March 1, 2019
C. February 1, 2019 D. December 31, 2018

39. What is the TOTAL interest that will be earned on the note? 39.____

A. $27 B. $270 C. $108 D. $10.80

40. What interest will be earned on the note for the old accounting period (December 1-31)? 40.____

A. $90 B. $36 C. $9 D. $3.60

KEY (CORRECT ANSWERS)

1. D	11. C	21. C	31. B
2. C	12. A	22. B	32. D
3. B	13. B	23. D	33. C
4. A	14. D	24. B	34. D
5. D	15. A	25. D	35. A
6. C	16. C	26. A	36. C
7. B	17. B	27. B	37. B
8. A	18. C	28. B	38. B
9. B	19. D	29. C	39. A
10. D	20. A	30. D	40. C

TEST 2

DIRECTIONS: Each question or incomplete statement is followed by several suggested answers or completions. Select the one that BEST answers the question or completes the statement. *PRINT THE LETTER OF THE CORRECT ANSWER IN THE SPACE AT THE RIGHT.*

Questions 1-4.

DIRECTIONS: Questions 1 through 4 are to be answered on the basis of the following information, to be included in a deposit slip.

14 twenty dollar bills	63 quarters
52 ten dollar bills	22 dimes
12 five dollar bills	44 nickels
43 one dollar bills	70 pennies

Checks: $236.34 and $129.72

1. What is the TOTAL amount of currency for this deposit? 1.____

   A. $923.85 B. $1269.06 C. $903.00 D. $1299.91

2. What is the TOTAL amount of coin for this deposit? 2.____

   A. $20.85 B. $923.85 C. $903.00 D. $1299.91

3. What is the TOTAL amount of check for this deposit? 3.____

   A. $20.85 B. $366.06 C. $1299.91 D. $903.00

4. What is the TOTAL deposit for this slip? 4.____

   A. $1269.06 B. $903.00 C. $923.85 D. $1289.91

Questions 5-7.

DIRECTIONS: Questions 5 through 7 are to be answered on the basis of the following information.

Angela Martinez's last check stub balance was $675.50. Her bank statement balance dated April 30 was $652.00. A $250 deposit was in transit on that date. Outstanding checks were as follows: No. 127, $65.00; No. 129, $203.50; No. 130, $50.00. The bank service charge for the month was $5.00.

5. What was Angela Martinez's available checkbook balance on April 30? 5.____

   A. $652.00 B. $338.50 C. $583.50 D. $675.50

6. In order to reconcile her checkbook balance with her bank statement balance, what must Angela Martinez do? 6.____

   A. Add her checkbook balance to the balance on her bank statement
   B. Subtract her checkbook balance from the balance on her bank statement

C. Ignore her checkbook balance and adopt the balance on her bank statement
D. Adjust the checkbook balance by adding deposits and debiting outstanding checks and charges

7. The check stub balance referred to in the problem refers to the 7.____

A. last check Angela Martinez recorded in her checkbook
B. amount of money left in Angela Martinez's account according to her own calculations based on the checks, charges, and deposits she has written and recorded
C. amount of money left in Angela Martinez's account according to the bank's calculations based on the checks, charges, and deposits posted to her account
D. number of checks left in her checkbook

Questions 8-9.

DIRECTIONS: Questions 8 and 9 are to be answered on the basis of the following information.

Tu Nguyen, an interior designer, received his June bank statement on July 2. The balance was $622.66. His last check stub balance was $700. On comparing the two, he noticed that a deposit of $275 made on June 30 was not included on the statement; also, a bank service charge of $4 was deducted. Outstanding checks were as follows: No. 331, $97.50; No. 332, $207; No. 335, $25.40; and No. 336, $68.97.

8. What is Nguyen's CORRECT available bank balance? 8.____

A. $494.79 B. $897.66 C. $700.00 D. $219.79

9. The bank statement balance referred to in the problem refers to the 9.____

A. last check Tu Nguyen recorded in his checkbook
B. last check presented for payment to Tu Nguyen's account
C. amount of money left in Tu Nguyen's account according to the bank's calculations based on the checks, charges, and deposits posted to his account
D. amount of money left in Tu Nguyen's account based on his own calculations of the checks, charges, and deposits he has written and recorded

10. What of the following endorsements would be an example of a simple Endorsement in Blank? 10.____

A. Pay to the Order of Joanie Anderson
B. Joanie Anderson
C. For deposit only; Acct. No. 12345; Joanie Anderson
D. Without Recourse; Joanie Anderson

11. Which of the following endorsements would limit the further purpose or use of the endorsed check? 11.____

A. Pay to the Order of Joanie Anderson
B. Joanie Anderson
C. For deposit only; Acct. No. 12345; Joanie Anderson,
D. Without Recourse; Joanie Anderson

12. Which of the following endorsements would protect the endorser from legal responsibility for payment, should the drawer have insufficient funds to honor his/her own check? 12.____

A. Pay to the Order of Joanie Anderson
B. Joanie Anderson
C. For deposit only; Acct. No. 12345; Joanie Anderson
D. Without Recourse; Joanie Anderson

Questions 13-24.

DIRECTIONS: Questions 13 - 24 are to be answered on the basis of the following ledger accounts for Wheelsmith Organic Farms.

Wheelsmith Organic Farms
Ledger Accounts

Cash

Jan. 1 4,000	

Accounts Payable

	Jan. 1 2,000

Service Supplies

Jan. 1 2,000	

Shelley Wheelsmith, Capital

	Jan. 1 11,000

Machinery

Jan. 1 7,000	

13. Transaction #1: On January 5, Shelley Wheelsmith, the proprietor, received cash amounting to $5,000 as a result of returning machinery that had recently been purchased. What account(s) should this transaction be posted to? 13.____

A. Cash
B. Cash and Machinery
C. Machinery
D. Cash, Machinery, and Service Supplies

14. Transaction #2: On January 8, Shelley Wheelsmith, the proprietor, sent out a check for $600 in partial payment of the accounts payable.
What account(s) should this transaction be posted to? 14.____

A. Accounts Payable
B. Accounts Payable and Cash
C. Accounts Payable and Capital
D. Cash

15. Transaction #3: On January 14, Shelley Wheelsmith, proprietor, made an additional investment in the business by contributing machinery valued at $1,500.
What account(s) should this transaction be posted to? 15.____

A. Machinery
B. Machinery and Capital
C. Capital
D. Machinery and Cash

16. Transaction #4: On January 26, Shelley Wheelsmith, proprietor, purchased additional service supplies for $200. She agreed to pay the obligation in 30 days. What account(s) should this transaction be posted to? 16.____

A. Accounts Payable and Liabilities
B. Service supplies
C. Accounts Payable
D. Accounts Payable and Service supplies

17. Transaction #5: On January 31, Shelley Wheelsmith, proprietor, purchased service supplies paying cash of $50. What account(s) should this transaction be posted to? 17.____

A. Service supplies
B. Service supplies and Accounts Payable
C. Cash and Service supplies
D. Cash

18. What is the balance in the Cash account after all of these transactions are posted? 18.____

A. $9,000 B. $1,000 C. $5,000 D. $8,350

19. What is the balance in the Machinery account after all of these transactions are posted? 19.____

A. $7,000 B. $5,000 C. $3,500 D. $13,500

20. What is the balance in the Accounts Payable account after all of these transactions are posted? 20.____

A. $800 B. $600 C. $2,600 D. $1,600

21. What is the balance in the Capital account after all of these transactions are posted? 21.____

A. $12,500 B. $800 C. $11,600 D. $10,400

22. What is the balance in the Service supplies account after all of these transactions are posted? 22.____

A. $2,000 B. $2,250 C. $750 D. $2,200

23. What are the total assets of Wheelsmith Organic Farms after these transactions have been posted? 23.____

A. $10,600 B. $11,850 C. $14,100 D. $10,750

24. What are the total liabilities and capital for Wheelsmith Organic Farms after these transactions have been posted? 24.____

A. $14,100 B. $12,500 C. $11,850 D. $10,600

Questions 25-28.

DIRECTIONS: Questions 25 through 28 are to be answered on the basis of the following information.

At the end of an accounting period, Andy's Framing Gallery recorded the following information: Sales, $125,225; Merchandise Inventory, December 31, $95,325; Purchases Returns and Allowances, $3,500; Merchandise Inventory, January 1, $98,725; Freight on Purchases, $2,500; Purchases, $120,000.

25. What are the net purchases for Andy's Framing Gallery during the accounting period? 25.____

A. $120,000 B. $119,000 C. $3,500 D. $122,500

26. What is the cost of goods available for sale? 26.____

A. $119,000 B. $98,725 C. $95,325 D. $217,725

27. What is the total cost of goods sold for this accounting period? 27.____

A. $217,725 B. $95,325 C. $122,400 D. $125,225

28. What is the gross profit on sales for this accounting period? 28.____

A. $2825 B. $2500 C. $125,225 D. $122,400

Questions 29-40.

DIRECTIONS: Questions 29 through 40 are to be answered on the basis of the following information.

The Joie de Vivre Co. received the promissory notes listed below during the last quarter of its calendar year:

	Date	Face Amount	Terms	Interest Rate	Date Discounted	Discount Rate
(1)	10/8	$3,600	30 days	-	10/18	9%
(2)	9/22	$8,000	60 days	6%	10/1	7%
(3)	11/15	$3,000	90 days	7%	11/20	8%

29. What is the due date for the first note? 29.____

A. 12/31 B. 11/7 C. 12/7 D. 10/31

30. What interest will be due when the first note matures? 30.____

A. $3 B. $3,600 C. $30 D. $0

31. What is the maturity value of the first note? 31.____

A. $3,600 B. $3,630 C. $0 D. $3,603

32. What is the discount period for the first note? 32.____

A. One fiscal year
B. 10 days
C. 20 days
D. One month

33. What is the due date for the second note? 33.____

A. 12/21 B. 11/21 C. 10/21 D. 1/21

34. What interest will be due when the second note matures? 34.____

A. $60 B. $800.00 C. $8.00 D. $80.00

35. What is the maturity value of the second note? 35.____

A. $8,000 B. $8,080 C. $8,800 D. $8,008

36. What is the discount period for the second note? 36.____

A. 51 days B. 10 days C. 360 days D. 60 days

37. What is the due date for the third note? 37.____

A. 1/14 B. 12/15 C. 12/31 D. 2/13

38. What interest will be due when the third note matures? 38.____

A. $5.25 B. $52.50 C. $525 D. $90

39. What is the maturity value of the third note? 39.____

A. $3525 B. $3005.25 C. $3052.50 D. $3090

40. What is the discount period for the third note? 40.____

A. 60 days B. 85 days C. 5 days D. 90 days

KEY (CORRECT ANSWERS)

1. C	11. C	21. A	31. A
2. A	12. D	22. B	32. C
3. B	13. B	23. C	33. B
4. D	14. B	24. A	34. D
5. C	15. B	25. B	35. B
6. D	16. D	26. D	36. A
7. B	17. C	27. C	37. D
8. A	18. D	28. A	38. B
9. C	19. C	29. B	39. C
10. B	20. D	30. D	40. B

TEST 3

DIRECTIONS: Each question or incomplete statement is followed by several suggested answers or completions. Select the one that BEST answers the question or completes the statement. *PRINT THE LETTER OF THE CORRECT ANSWER IN THE SPACE AT THE RIGHT.*

Questions 1-8.

DIRECTIONS: Questions 1 through 8 are to be answered on the basis of the following Balance Sheet.

Laura Lee's Bridal Shop
Balance Sheet
December 31, 2018

Assets		
Cash	$14,000	
Accounts Receivable	3,000	
Bridal Accessories	10,000	
Gowns and Other Inventory	30,000	
Total Assets		$57,000
Liabilities and Capital		
Accounts Payable	$ 4,000	
Notes Payable	28,000	
Total Liabilities		$32,000
Laura Lee, Capital		25,000
Total Liabilities and Capital		$57,000

1. When was the balance sheet prepared? 1.____

    A. January 2019
    B. December 31, 2018
    C. After the close of the 2018 fiscal year
    D. December 1, 2018

2. How does the date on this balance sheet differ from the date on the statement of capital or income statement? 2.____

    A. It doesn't differ. The dates for each statement signify the same time period.
    B. The date on a balance sheet represents the period during which any changes indicated on the statement took place, whereas the other financial statements represent the moment in time when the statement was prepared.
    C. The date on a balance sheet represents the moment in time when the statement was prepared, whereas the other financial statements represent the period during which any changes indicated on the statement took place.
    D. The date on a balance sheet indicates an entire year, whereas the dates on the other statements indicate a single month.

3. Can Laura Lee purchase more bridal gowns for the business paying cash of $16,000? 3.____

    A. *No*, because the business has only $14,000 cash available
    B. *Yes*, because the business has $57,000 cash available
    C. *Yes*, because the business has $57,000 available in assets
    D. *No*, because the business has $57,000 in liabilities

4. What is the owner's equity of Laura Lee's Bridal Shop? 4.____
Since total equity consists of total ______, total equity is ______.

A. assets minus total liabilities and proprietor's capital; $0
B. assets minus total liabilities; $25,000
C. assets; $57,000
D. liabilities and proprietor's capital; $57,000

5. What is the TOTAL amount of Laura Lee's claim against the total assets of the business? 5.____

A. $57,000 B. $25,000 C. $0 D. $39,000

6. What is the amount of the creditors' claims against the assets of the business? 6.____

A. $4,000 B. $57,000 C. $32,000 D. $28,000

7. What is the net income for the period? 7.____

A. $57,000
B. $0
C. $25,000
D. This information cannot be obtained from the balance sheet

8. What was the value of Laura Lee's ownership in this business on January 1, 2004? 8.____

A. $25,000
B. $57,000
C. $14,000
D. This information cannot be obtained from the balance sheet

Questions 9-21.

DIRECTIONS: Each of the transactions described in Questions 9 through 21 occurred within an accounting period. For each question, indicate which of the four journals the transaction would be recorded in.

9. Sale of goods on account 9.____

A. Cash receipts B. Cash payments
C. General D. Sales

10. Cash payment of a promissory note 10.____

A. Cash payments B. Cash receipts
C. Sales D. General

11. Received a credit memo from a creditor 11.____

A. Purchases B. General
C. Sales D. Cash payments

12. Sale of merchandise for cash 12.____

A. Purchases B. General
C. Cash receipts D. Cash payments

13. Received a check from a customer in partial payment of an oral agreement 13.____

A. Purchases B. Sales
C. General D. Cash receipts

14. Issued a credit memo to a customer 14.____

A. Purchases B. General
C. Cash payments D. Sales

15. Received a promissory note in place of an oral agreement from a customer 15.____

A. General B. Cash payments
C. Cash receipts D. Sales

16. Paid monthly rent 16.____

A. General B. Purchases
C. Cash payments D. Cash receipts

17. Sale of a service on credit 17.____

A. Cash receipts B. General
C. Purchases D. Sales

18. Purchase of office furniture on credit 18.____

A. General B. Purchases
C. Cash payments D. Cash receipts

19. Purchased merchandise for cash 19.____

A. Cash payments B. Cash receipts
C. Sales D. General

20. Cash refund to a customer 20.____

A. Cash receipts B. Sales
C. General D. Cash payments

21. Purchases made on credit 21.____

A. Purchases B. Sales
C. Cash receipts D. General

Questions 22-26.

DIRECTIONS: Questions 22 through 26 are to be answered on the basis of the following inventory, purchased by International Soap and Candle Traders, Inc.

700 units at $4.50, 320 units at $3.75, 550 units at $2.75, and 475 units at $1.90

22. Calculate the total price of the units that cost $4.50. 22.____

A. $315 B. $31,500 C. $3,150 D. $2,800

23. Calculate the total price of the units that cost $3.75. 23.____

A. $2062.50 B. $12,000 C. $120 D. $1,200

24. Calculate the total price of the units that cost $2.75. 24.____

A. $1,512.50 B. $15,125 C. $151.25 D. $550

25. Calculate the total price of the units that cost $1.90. 25.____

A. $90.25 B. $9025 C. $902.50 D. $475

26. Calculate the average cost per unit. 26.____

A. $27 B. $33.10 C. $0.30 D. $3.31

27. The interest on a promissory note is recorded at which of the following times? 27.____

A. When the debt is incurred
B. At the end of the accounting period
C. When the note is paid
D. At the beginning of each month

28. The interest on a promissory note begins accruing at which of the following times? 28.____

A. When the debt is incurred
B. At the end of the accounting period
C. When the note is paid
D. At the beginning of each month

29. The maturity value of an interest-bearing note is the 29.____

A. interest accrued on the note plus a service charge imposed by the lender
B. interest accrued on the note
C. face value of the note
D. principal of the note plus interest

30. A cash receipts journal is used to record the 30.____

A. number of cash sales a business makes
B. number of credit sales a business makes
C. collection of cash made by the business
D. expenditure of cash made by the business

31. Calculate the interest on a promissory note issued for $3,000 at an interest rate of 8%, due in 360 days. (Assume a banking year of 360 days.) 31.____

A. $300 B. $240 C. $60 D. $360

32. Calculate the total payment due for a promissory note issued for $1,000 at an interest rate of 10%, due in 90 days. (Assume a banking year of 360 days.) 32.____

A. $25 B. $1050 C. $1000 D. $1025

33. Calculate the total payment due for a promissory note issued for $5,000 at an interest rate of 6%, due in 60 days. (Assume a banking year of 360 days.) 33.____

A. $5,050 B. $50 C. $5,000 D. $5,300

34. Calculate the interest on a promissory note issued for $1,700 at an interest rate of 12%, due in 45 days. (Assume a banking year of 360 days.) 34.____

A. $204 B. $1725.50 C. $25.50 D. $1904

35. Calculate the interest on a promissory note issued for $600 at an interest rate of 9%, due in 90 days. (Assume a banking year of 360 days.) 35.____

A. $13.50 B. $135 C. $54 D. $540

KEY (CORRECT ANSWERS)

1.	B	16.	C
2.	C	17.	D
3.	A	18.	B
4.	B	19.	A
5.	B	20.	D
6.	C	21.	A
7.	D	22.	C
8.	D	23.	D
9.	D	24.	A
10.	A	25.	C
11.	B	26.	D
12.	C	27.	C
13.	D	28.	A
14.	B	29.	D
15.	A	30.	C

31. B
32. D
33. A
34. C
35. A

EXAMINATION SECTION
TEST 1

DIRECTIONS: Each question or incomplete statement is followed by several suggested answers or completions. Select the one that BEST answers the question or completes the statement. *PRINT THE LETTER OF THE CORRECT ANSWER IN THE SPACE AT THE RIGHT.*

Questions 1-12.

DIRECTIONS: Questions 1 through 12 refer to the following information.

At the Supreme Plastic Company, located in Detroit, employees are paid bi-weekly. Their paychecks are calculated on the following deductions from their gross pay:

a. Federal and State tax combined is 14%
b. City tax of 3%, only for Detroit residents
c. Union dues for union members only. The union dues are calculated as follows: 1.5% of an employee's gross pay or $15, <u>whichever is smaller</u>
d. Medical coverage, which is calculated as follows: 2% of gross pay for employees under the age of 30, and 3.5% of gross pay for employees 30 years of age or older.

1. Charlie's gross pay per paycheck is $840. He lives outside Detroit, is not a union member, and is 36 years old. What is his net pay? 1.____

   A. $680.40 B. $693.00 C. $705.60 D. $718.20 E. $730.80

2. Diane's gross pay per paycheck is $920. She lives in Detroit, is not a union member, and is 29 years old. What is her net pay? 2.____

   A. $782.00 B. $772.80 C. $763.60 D. $754.40 E. $745.20

3. Barney's gross pay per paycheck is $1030. He lives outside Detroit, is a union member, and is 25 years old. What is his net pay? 3.____

   A. $850.20 B. $857.70 C. $865.20 D. $872.70 E. $880.20

4. Vanessa's gross pay per paycheck is $980. She lives in Detroit, is a union member, and is 40 years old. What is her net pay? 4.____

   A. $749.70 B. $757.05 C. $764.40 D. $771.75 E. $779.10

5. Fred's gross pay per paycheck is $750. He lives in Detroit, is a union member, and is 30 years old. What is his net pay? 5.____

   A. $607.50 B. $596.25 C. $585.00 D. $573.75 E. $562.50

6. Christine lives outside Detroit, is not a union member, and is 23 years old. Her net pay per paycheck is $567.00. What is her gross pay? 6.____

   A. $662.50 B. $675.00 C. $687.50 D. $700.00 E. $712.50

7. Marie lives in Detroit, is not a union member, and is 33 years old. Her net pay per paycheck is $890.40. 7.____
What is her gross pay?

A. $1060.00 B. $1080.00 C. $1100.00
D. $1120.00 E. $1140.00

8. Todd lives outside Detroit, is a union member, and is 45 years old. His net pay per paycheck is $607.82. 8.____
What is his gross pay?

A. $779.60 B. $772.30 C. $765.00 D. $757.70 E. $750.40

9. Priscilla lives in Detroit, is a union member, and is 27 years old. Her net pay per paycheck is $981.46. 9.____
What is her gross pay?

A. $1246.80 B. $1238.50 C. $1230.20
D. $1221.90 E. $1213.60

10. During the first two-week pay period in May, Floyd was a Detroit resident and not a union member. As of the second two-week pay period in May, he moved out of Detroit and joined the company union. 10.____
If his gross pay per paycheck remained at $1300, how much was the *increase* in net pay?

A. $15.00 B. $19.50 C. $24.00 D. $28.50 E. $33.00

11. During the first two-week pay period in July, Paula was not a Detroit resident, but was a union member. As of the second two-week pay period in July, she moved to Detroit and left the company union. 11.____
If her gross pay per paycheck remained at $880, how much was the *decrease* in net pay?

A. $9.60 B. $10.50 C. $11.40 D. $12.30 E. $13.20

12. Roger is a 50-year-old employee. During the first two-week pay period in August, he carried medical insurance. Due to financial hardship, he was allowed to drop this coverage as of the second two-week pay period. The net pay on his second paycheck was $18.92 higher than that of his first paycheck. 12.____
What is his gross pay?

A. $524.10 B. $529.60 C. $535.10 D. $540.60 E. $546.10

Questions 13-25.

DIRECTIONS: Questions 13 through 25 refer to the following information.

At the Lucky Star Restaurant, employees are paid weekly. Their paychecks are calculated on the following deductions from their gross pay (salary earnings):

a. Federal and State tax combined is applied to salary earnings only (not including tips) in the following manner: 12% of salary up to and including a weekly salary of $400, plus 10% of any salary in excess of $400
b. Tax on tips. This is calculated on <u>the larger of</u> $3 or 2% of tips collected.

c. Medical coverage, which is optional. The amount deducted is as shown in this chart:

Employee's Age (Yrs)	Employee's Years of Service		
	Less Than 1 Year	1-5 Years	Over 5 Years
18-30	$5	$4	$3
31-40	$9	$7	$5
Over 40	$13	$10	$7

NOTE: Net pay <u>will include</u> the tips earned, if the person involved did earn tips.

13. Frank's gross pay per paycheck is $380, including tips. In a particular week, he receives $50 in tips. 13.____
If he has no medical coverage, what is his net pay?

A. $387.40 B. $385.40 C. $383.40 D. $381.40 E. $379.40

14. Gina's gross pay per paycheck is $460, excluding tips. In a particular week, she receives $70 in tips. 14.____
If she has no medical coverage, what is her net pay?

A. $461.00 B. $467.00 C. $473.00 D. $479.00 E. $485.00

15. Cliff's gross pay per paycheck is $510, excluding tips. In a particular week, he receives $180 in tips. 15.____
If he has no medical coverage, what is his net pay?

A. $627.40 B. $638.00 C. $648.60 D. $659.20 E. $669.80

16. Diane's gross pay per paycheck is $350, excluding tips. In a particular week, she receives $200 in tips. 16.____
If she has no medical coverage, what is her net pay?

A. $506.00 B. $505.50 C. $505.00 D. $504.50 E. $504.00

17. Jean is a part-time cashier, earning a weekly salary of $320. She receives no tips, but does carry medical coverage. 17.____
If she is 23 years old and has 4 years of service, what is her net pay?

A. $275.60 B. $277.60 C. $279.60 D. $281.60 E. $283.60

18. Pete is a part-time cook, earning a weekly salary of $440. He receives no tips, but does carry medical coverage. 18.____
If he is 42 years old and has 8 years of service, what is his net pay?

A. $377.80 B. $378.60 C. $379.40 D. $380.20 E. $381.00

19. Melissa is a waitress, earning a weekly salary of $560, excluding tips. During one week, she receives $130 in tips. 19.____
If she has medical coverage, is 36 years old, and has 5 years of service, what is her net pay?

A. $613.00 B. $616.00 C. $619.00 D. $622.00 E. $625.00

20. Henry is a part-time waiter, earning a weekly salary of $350, excluding tips. During one week, he receives $90 in tips. 20.____
If he has medical coverage, is 32 years old, and has 7 months of service, what is his net pay?

A. $386.00 B. $388.00 C. $390.00 D. $392.00 E. $394.00

21. During the first week of November, Roseanne was a waitress, earning a weekly salary of $570, plus $140 in tips. During the second week of November, her weekly salary was increased by 6% and her tips rose by 10%. What was her total net pay for these two weeks? (Assume no medical coverage for either week.) 21.____

A. $1311.90 B. $1317.50 C. $1323.10
D. $1328.70 E. $1334.30

22. During the first week of October, Don was a waiter, earning a weekly salary of $610, plus $100 in tips. He had no medical coverage at that time. During the second week of October, he was promoted to an Assistant Manager with a weekly salary of $800 and no tips. He also carried medical coverage. During that time frame, he had 4 years of service and was 52 years old. 22.____
What was his total net pay for these weeks?

A. $1320.00 B. $1325.00 C. $1330.00
D. $1335.00 E. $1340.00

23. Arlene is a waitress, 46 years old, with 10 months of service. During one particular week, she had $50 in tips and net pay of $305.04. 23.____
If she has medical coverage, what is her gross pay, excluding tips?

A. $296.00 B. $302.00 C. $308.00 D. $314.00 E. $320.00

24. Francine is the restaurant's bookkeeper. She is 39 years old with 10 years of service. She carries medical coverage and her weekly salary includes no tips. 24.____
If her net pay per week is $869.45, what is her gross pay?

A. $980.50 B. $978.10 C. $975.70 D. $973.30 E. $970.90

25. Ray is the chief waiter. He is 60 years old with 20 years of service. He carries medical coverage and his gross weekly salary, excluding tips, is $750. Assuming his weekly tips exceed $150, if his net pay (including salary and tips) is $934.40, how much does he earn in tips? 25.____

A. $271.00 B. $274.00 C. $277.00 D. $280.00 E. $283.00

KEY (CORRECT ANSWERS)

1. B
2. E
3. A
4. C
5. C
6. B
7. D
8. E
9. C
10. C
11. E
12. D
13. D
14. C
15. A
16. E
17. B
18. E
19. B
20. A
21. D
22. E
23. C
24. A
25. D

SOLUTIONS TO PROBLEMS

1. CORRECT ANSWER: B
Net pay = \$840 - (.14)(840) - (.035)(840) = \$693.00

2. CORRECT ANSWER: E
Net pay = \$920 - (.14)(920) - (.03)(920) - (.02)(920) = \$745.20

3. CORRECT ANSWER: A
Net pay = \$1030 - (.14)(1030) - 15 - (.02)(1030) = \$850.20

4. CORRECT ANSWER: C
Net pay = \$980 - (.14)(980) - (.03)(980) - (.015)(980) - (.035)(980) = \$764.40

5. CORRECT ANSWER: C
Net pay = \$750 - (.14)(750) - (.03)(750) - (.015)(750) - (.035)(750) = \$585.00

6. CORRECT ANSWER: B
Let x = gross pay. Then, x - .14x - .02x = \$567.00
Simplifying, .84x = 567.00, so x - \$675.00

7. CORRECT ANSWER: D
Let x = gross pay. Then, x - .14x - .03x - .035x = \$890.40. Simplifying, .795x = 890.40, so x = \$1120.00

8. CORRECT ANSWER: E
Let x = gross pay. Then, x - .14x - .015x - .035x = \$607.82. Simplifying, .81x = 607.82, so x = \$750.40

9. CORRECT ANSWER: C
Let x = gross pay. Then, x - .14x - .03x - \$15 - .02x = \$981.46.
Simplifying, .81x = 996.46, so x = \$1230.20. NOTE: Her union dues were \$15, not 1.5% of her gross pay because 1.5% of 1230.20 is \$18.45, which exceeds \$15.

10. CORRECT ANSWER: C
His net pay was affected by a \$15 decrease due to union dues, but also by a (.03)(\$1300) = \$39 increase due to moving out of Detroit. Finally, \$39 - \$15 = \$24

11. CORRECT ANSWER: E
Her net pay was affected by a (.015)(\$880) = \$13.20 increase due to the removal of union dues, and also by a (.03)(\$880) = \$26.40 decrease due to a Detroit city tax. Thus, her net pay was decreased by \$26.40 - \$13.20 = \$13.20.

12. CORRECT ANSWER: D
His medical coverage represents 3.5% of his gross pay. If his gross pay = x, then .035x = \$18.92. Solving, x \$540.60

13. CORRECT ANSWER: D
Net pay = \$430 - (.12)(380) - 3 = \$331.40

14. CORRECT ANSWER: C
Net pay = \$530 - (.12)(400) - (.10)(60) - 3 = \$473.00

15. CORRECT ANSWER: A
Net pay = \$690 - (.12)(400) - (.10)(110) - (.02)(180) = \$627.40

16. CORRECT ANSWER: E
Net pay = \$550 - (.12)(350) - (.02)(200) = \$504.00

17. CORRECT ANSWER: B
Net pay = \$320 - (.12)(320) - 4 = \$277.60

18. CORRECT ANSWER: E
Net pay = \$440 - (.12)(400) - (.10)(40) - 7 = \$381.00

19. CORRECT ANSWER: B
Net pay = \$690 - (.12)(400) - (.10)(160) - 3 - 7 = \$486.00

20. CORRECT ANSWER: A
Net pay = \$440 - (.12)(350) - 3 - 9 = \$386.00

21. CORRECT ANSWER: D
First week net pay = \$710 - (.12)(400) - (.10)(170) - 3 = \$642.00
Second week net pay = \$758.20 - (.12)(400) - (.10) (204.20) - (154)(.02) = \$686.70
Total net pay = \$1328.70

22. CORRECT ANSWER: E
First week net pay = \$710 - (.12)(400) - (.10)(210) - 3 = \$638.00
Second week net pay = \$800 - (.12)(400) - (.10)(400) - 10 = \$702.00
Total net pay = \$1340.00

23. CORRECT ANSWER: C
Let x = gross pay, excluding tips. Then, we have: x + 50 -.12x - 3 - 13 = \$305.04. This simplifes to .88x = 271.04.
Solving, x - \$308.00

24. CORRECT ANSWER: A
Let x = gross pay. Then, x - (.12)(400) - (.10)(x-400) - 5 = \$869.45. Simplifying, x - 48 - .10x + 40 - 5 = 869.45. Then, .90x = 882.45.
Solving, x - \$980.50

25. CORRECT ANSWER: D
Let x = tips earned. Then, \$750 + x - (400)(.12) - (350)(.10) - .02x - 7 = 934.40.
Simplifying, .98x + 660 = 934.40.
Solving, x = \$280.00

TEST 2

DIRECTIONS: Each question or incomplete statement is followed by several suggested answers or completions. Select the one that BEST answers the question or completes the statement. *PRINT THE LETTER OF THE CORRECT ANSWER IN THE SPACE AT THE RIGHT.*

Questions 1-13.

DIRECTIONS: Questions 1 through 13 refer to the following information.

At the Stretch-Tight Rubber Band Company, employees are paid on the 15th day and the last day of every month. Their paychecks are calculated based on the following deductions from their gross pay:

a. Federal tax of 12%
b. State tax of 7%
c. Union dues for union members only. The union dues are calculated as follows: .5% for up to 1 year of employment; 1% for more than 1 year but no more than 5 years of employment; 1.5% for more than 5 years of employment.

1. Jack's gross pay per paycheck is $1000. If he is NOT a union member, what is his net pay? 1.____

A. $930 B. $880 C. $810 D. $720 E. $640

2. Robin's gross pay per paycheck is $900. If she is a union member with 3 years of employment, what is her net pay? 2.____

A. $720 B. $729 C. $738 D. $747 E. $756

3. Suzanne's gross pay per paycheck is $1200. If she is a union member with 6 years of employment, what is her net pay? 3.____

A. $1008 B. $990 C. $972 D. $954 E. $936

4. Mike's gross pay per paycheck is $1600. If he is a union member with 5 months of employment, what is his net pay? 4.____

A. $1240 B. $1248 C. $1264 D. $1280 E. $1288

5. For the month of May, Bonnie was not a union member up through May 15th, but became a union member on May 16th. She has 8 years of employment, and her gross pay per paycheck is $860. 5.____
What is her TOTAL net pay for May?

A. $1347.50 B. $1354.10 C. $1367.40
D. $1380.30 E. $1393.20

6. For the month of June, Bob was not a union member up through June 15th, but became a union member on June 16th. He has 4 years of employment, and his gross pay per paycheck is $700. 6.____
What is his TOTAL net pay for June?

A. $1135 B. $1127 C. $1120 D. $1112 E. $1104

7. Alice is not a union member and her net pay per paycheck is $761.40. What is her gross pay? 7.____

A. $860 B. $900 C. $940 D. $1000 E. $1060

8. Paul is a union member with 3 months of employment. If his net pay per paycheck is $627.90, what is his gross pay? 8.____

A. $760 B. $765 C. $770 D. $775 E. $780

9. Linda is a union member with 7 years of employment. If her net pay per paycheck is $898.35, what is her gross pay? 9.____

A. $1130 B. $1140 C. $1150 D. $1160 E. $1170

10. Ralph is a union member with 2 years of employment. If his net pay per paycheck is $1136, what is his gross pay? 10.____

A. $1438 B. $1420 C. $1410 D. $1402 E. $1388

11. Mary is a union member, and at the end of July of this year, she will have completed 1 year of employment. Her gross pay per paycheck in July is $1050, but beginning in August her gross pay (per paycheck) will become $1180.
What will be the *increase* in her net pay from July to August? 11.____

A. $86.40 B. $98.75 C. $112.45 D. $130.00 E. $143.35

12. Steve is a union member, and at the end of March of this year, he will have completed 5 years of employment. His gross pay per paycheck in March is $980, but beginning in April his gross pay (per paycheck) will become $1100.
What will be the *increase* in his net pay from March to April? 12.____

A. $62.50 B. $73.00 C. $84.50 D. $90.50 E. $96.00

13. Sherry has been a union member up through September of this year. She has 8 months of employment, and her gross pay per paycheck is $800. Beginning in October, she will become a non-union member, and her gross pay (per paycheck) will drop to $660.
What will be the *decrease* in her net pay from September to October? 13.____

A. $109.40 B. $110.80 C. $112.70 D. $113.40 E. $115.60

Questions 14-25.

DIRECTIONS: Questions 14 through 25 refer to the following information.

At the Iron-Clad Steel Company, employees are paid weekly. Their paychecks are calculated based on the following deductions from their gross pay:

a. Federal tax and State tax combined is 16%
b. Union dues for union members only. The union dues are calculated as follows: 2% of an employee's gross pay, up to and including a gross pay of $500, plus of any gross pay in excess of $500.
c. Medical coverage, which is calculated as follows, based on the employee's age: 1.5% of gross pay for employees age 18 through 25; 2.5% of gross pay for employees age 26 through 39; and 5% for employees age 40 or older.

14. Bill's gross pay per paycheck is $820. If he is 24 years old and is not a union member, what is his net pay? 14.____

A. $651.90 B. $664.20 C. $676.50 D. $688.80 E. $701.10

15. Debra's gross pay per paycheck is $740. If she is 41 years old and is not a union member, what is her net pay? 15.____

A. $620.40 B. $602.50 C. $584.60 D. $566.70 E. $548.80

16. Mark's gross pay per paycheck is $700. If he is 32 years old and a union member, what is his net pay? 16.____

A. $564.50 B. $562.50 C. $560.50 D. $558.50 E. $556.50

17. Virginia's gross pay per paycheck is $490. If she is 19 years old and a union member, what is her net pay? 17.____

A. $378.85 B. $382.75 C. $386.65 D. $390.55 E. $394.45

18. Rhonda's gross pay per paycheck is $650. If she is 45 years old and a union member, what is her net pay? 18.____

A. $485.75 B. $502.00 C. $518.25 D. $534.50 E. $550.75

19. For the first week in June, Marianne was not a union member, but became a union member at the beginning of the second week. Her gross pay per paycheck is $880, and she is 38 years old.
What is her TOTAL net pay for these two weeks? 19.____

A. $1448.20 B. $1441.30 C. $1434.40
D. $1427.50 E. $1420.60

20. For the first week in January, Carl was not a union member, but became a union member at the beginning of the second week. His gross pay per paycheck is $470, and he is 22 years old.
What is his TOTAL net pay for these two weeks? 20.____

A. $766.10 B. $775.50 C. $784.90 D. $794.30 E. $803.70

21. Dave's gross pay per paycheck during the first week of October was $450, but his gross pay increased to $550 for the second week in October. If he is 50 years old and a union member, what is his TOTAL net pay for these two weeks? 21.____

A. $805.00 B. $793.50 C. $782.00 D. $770.50 E. $759.00

22. Nancy is not a union member and her net pay per paycheck is $513.45. If she is 35 years old, what is her gross pay? 22.____

A. $615 B. $620 C. $625 D. $630 E. $635

23. Phyllis is not a union member and her net pay per paycheck is $639.90. If she is 43 years old, what is her gross pay? 23.____

A. $780 B. $795 C. $810 D. $825 E. $840

24. Tom is a union member and his net pay per paycheck is $350.90. If he is 21 years old, what is his gross pay? 24.____

A. $436 B. $448 C. $460 D. $472 E. $484

25. Ron is a union member and his net pay per paycheck is $767.80. If he is 37 years old, what is his gross pay? 25.____

A. $972.50 B. $960.00 C. $947.50 D. $935.00 E. $922.50

KEY (CORRECT ANSWERS)

1.	C	11.	B
2.	A	12.	D
3.	D	13.	A
4.	E	14.	C
5.	D	15.	C
6.	B	16.	D
7.	C	17.	E
8.	E	18.	B
9.	A	19.	E
10.	B	20.	A

21.	D
22.	D
23.	C
24.	A
25.	B

SOLUTIONS TO PROBLEMS

1. CORRECT ANSWER: C
   Net pay = $1000 - (.12)(1000) - (.07)(1000) = $810

2. CORRECT ANSWER: A
   Net pay = $900 - (.12)(900) - (.07)(900) - (.01)(900) = $720

3. CORRECT ANSWER: D
   Net pay = $1200 - (.12)(1200) - (.07)(1200) - (.015)(1200) = $954

4. CORRECT ANSWER: E
   Net pay = $1600 - (.12)(1600) - (.07)(1600) - (.005)(1600) = $1288

5. CORRECT ANSWER: D
   Net pay = [$860 - (.12)(860) - (.07)(860)] + [$860 - (.12)(860) - (.07)(860) - (.015)(860)] = $1380.30

6. CORRECT ANSWER: B
   Net pay = [$700 - (.12)(700) - (.07)(700)] + [$700 - (.12)(700) - (.07)(700) - (.01)(700)] = $1127

7. CORRECT ANSWER: C
   Let x - gross pay. Then, x - .12x - .07x = 761.40, so .81x = 761.40. Solving, x = $940

8. CORRECT ANSWER: E
   Let x = gross pay. Then, x - .12x - .07x - .005x = 627.90
   So, .805x = 627.90. Solving, x = $780

9. CORRECT ANSWER: A
   Let x = gross pay. Then, x - .12x - .07x - .015x = 898.35,
   So .795x = 898.35.
   Solving, x $1130

10. CORRECT ANSWER: B
    Let x = gross pay. Then, x - .12x - .07x - .01x = 1136
    So, .80x = 1136. Solving, x = $1420

11. CORRECT ANSWER: B
    Mary's net pay in July = $1050 - (.12)(1050) - (.07)(1050) - (.005)(1050) = $845.25. Her net pay in August = $1180 -(.12)(1180) - (.07)(1180) - (.01)(1180) = $944.00
    Then, $944.00 - $845.25 = $98.75

12. CORRECT ANSWER: D
    Steve's net pay in March = $980 - (.12)(980) - (.07)(980)
    - (.01)(980) = 784.00. His net pay in April = $1100 - (.12)(1100)
    - (.07)(1100) - (.015)(1100) = $874.50. Then, $874.50 -$784.00 = $90.50

13. CORRECT ANSWER: A
Sherry's net pay in September = $800 - (.12)(800) - (.07)(800) - (.005)(800) - $644.00. Her net pay in October = $660 -(.12)(660) - (.07)(660) = $534.60. Then, $644.00 - $534.60 = $109.40

14. CORRECT ANSWER: C
Net pay = $820 - (.16)(820) - (.015)(820) = $676.50

15. CORRECT ANSWER: C
Net pay = $740 - (.16)(740) - (.05)(740) = $584.60

16. CORRECT ANSWER: D
Net pay = $700 - (.16)(700) - (.02)(500) - (.01)(200) -(.025)(700) = $558.50

17. CORRECT ANSWER: E
Net pay = $490 - (.16)(490) - (.02)(490) - (.015)(490) = $394.45

18. CORRECT ANSWER: B
Net pay = $650 - (.16)(650) - (.02)(500) - (.01)(150). -(.05)(650) = $502.00

19. CORRECT ANSWER: E
Net pay = [$880 - (.16)(880) - (.025)(880)] + [$880 - (.16)(880) - (.02)(500) - (.01)(380) - (.025)(880)] = $1420.60

20. CORRECT ANSWER: A
Net pay = [$470 - (.16)(470) - (.015)(470)] + [$470 - (.16)(470) - (.02)(470) - (.015)(470)] = $766.10

21. CORRECT ANSWER: D
Net pay = [$450 - (.16)(450) - (.02)(450) - (.05)(450)] + [$550 - (.16)(550) - (.02)(500) - (.01)(50) - (.05)(550)] = $770.50

22. CORRECT ANSWER: D
Let x - gross pay. Then, x - .16x - .025x = 513.45, so, .815x = 513.45. Solving, x = $630

23. CORRECT ANSWER: C
Let x = gross pay. Then, x - .16x - .05x = 639.90, so .79x - 639.90. Solving, x = $810

24. CORRECT ANSWER: A
Let x = gross pay. We can safely assume that his gross pay is less than $500, since all five selections are under $500. Then, x - .16x - .02x - .015x = 350.98, so, .805x = 350.98. Solving, x = $436

25. CORRECT ANSWER: B
Let x = gross pay. Since his gross pay must exceed $500, x - .16x - (.02) (500) - (.01)(x-500) - .025x = 767.80. Simplifying, .805x - 5 - 767.80. Solving, x - $960.00

BOOKKEEPING PROBLEMS
EXAMINATION SECTION
TEST 1

DIRECTIONS: Each question or incomplete statement is followed by several suggested answers or completions. Select the one that BEST answers the question or completes the statement. *PRINT THE LETTER OF THE CORRECT ANSWER IN THE SPACE AT THE RIGHT.*

1. The accounts in a general ledger are BEST arranged 1.____

   A. in numerical order
   B. according to the frequency with which each account is used
   C. according to the order in which the headings of the columns in the cash journals are arranged
   D. according to the order in which they are used in preparing financial statements

2. A physical inventory is an inventory obtained by 2.____

   A. an actual count of the items on hand
   B. adding the totals of the stock record cards
   C. deducting the cost of goods sold from the purchases for the period
   D. deducting the purchases from the sales for the period

3. Modern accounting practice favors the valuation of the inventories of a going concern at 3.____

   A. current market prices, if higher than cost
   B. cost or market, whichever is lower
   C. estimated selling price
   D. probable value at forced sale

4. A subsidiary ledger contains accounts which show 4.____

   A. details of contingent liabilities of undetermined amount
   B. totals of all asset accounts in the general ledger
   C. totals of all liability accounts in the general ledger
   D. details of an account in the general ledger

5. A statement of the assets, liabilities, and net worth of a business is called a 5.____

   A. trial balance
   B. budget
   C. profit and loss statement
   D. balance sheet

6. The one of the following which is NEVER properly considered a negotiable instrument is a(n) 6.____

   A. invoice
   B. bond
   C. promissory note
   D. endorsed check

7. The term *current assets* USUALLY includes such things as 7.____

   A. notes payable
   B. machinery and equipment
   C. furniture and fixtures
   D. accounts receivable

8. An accounting system which records revenues as soon as they are earned and records liabilities as soon as they are incurred regardless of the date of payment is said to operate on a(n) ______ basis. 8.___

A. accrual B. budgetary C. encumbrance D. cash

9. A *trial balance* is a list of 9.___

A. the credit balances in all accounts in a general ledger
B. all general ledger accounts and their balances
C. the asset accounts in a general ledger and their balances
D. the liability accounts in a general ledger and their balances

10. A controlling account contains the totals of 10.___

A. the accounts used in preparing the balance sheet at the end of the fiscal period
B. the individual amounts entered in the accounts of a subsidiary ledger during the fiscal period
C. all entries in the general journal during the fiscal period
D. the accounts used in preparing the profit and loss statement for the fiscal period

11. The ESSENTIAL nature of an asset is that it(s) 11.___

A. must be tangible
B. must be easily converted into cash
C. must have value
D. cost must be included in the profit and loss statement

12. When an asset is depreciated on the straight-line basis, the amount charged off for depreciation 12.___

A. is greater in the earlier years of the asset's life
B. is greater in the later years of the asset's life
C. varies each year according to the extent to which the asset is used during the year
D. is equal each full year of the asset's life

Questions 13-27.

DIRECTIONS: Questions 13 to 27 consist of a list of some of the accounts in a general ledger. Indicate whether each account listed generally contains a debit or a credit balance by putting the letter D (for debit balance) or the letter C (for credit balance) in the correspondingly numbered space on the right for each account listed. For example, for the account Cash, which generally contains a debit balance, you would give the letter D as your answer.

13. Sales Taxes Collected 13.___

14. Social Security Taxes Paid by Employer 14.___

15. Deposits from Customers 15.___

16. Freight Inward 16.___

17. Sales Discount 17.___

18. Withholding Taxes Payable 18.____

19. L. Norton, Drawings 19.____

20. Office Salaries 20.____

21. Merchandise Inventory 21.____

22. L. Norton, Capital 22.____

23. Purchases Returns 23.____

24. Unearned Rent Income 24.____

25. Reserve for Bad Debts 25.____

26. Depreciation of Machinery 26.____

27. Insurance Prepaid 27.____

Questions 28-42.

DIRECTIONS: Questions 28 to 42 consist of a list of some of the accounts in a general ledger. For the purpose of preparing financial statements, each of these accounts is to be classified into one of the following five major classifications, lettered A to E, as follows:

A. Assets B. Liabilities C. Proprietorship
D. Income E. Expense

You are to indicate the classification to which each account belongs by printing the correct letter, A, B, C, D, or E, in the correspondingly numbered space on the right. For example, for the account Furniture and Fixtures, which is an asset account, you would print the letter A.

28. Notes Receivable 28.____

29. Sales 29.____

30. Wages Payable 30.____

31. Office Salaries 31.____

32. Capital Stock Authorized 32.____

33. Goodwill 33.____

34. Capital Surplus 34.____

35. Office Supplies Used 35.____

36. Interest Payable 36.____

37. Prepaid Rent 37.____

38. Interest Cost 38.____

39. Accounts Payable 39.____

40. Prepaid Insurance 40.____

41. Merchandise Inventory 41.____

42. Interest Earned 42.____

43. A trial balance will NOT indicate that an error has been made in 43.____

A. computing the balance of an account
B. entering an amount in the wrong account
C. carrying forward the balance of an account
D. entering an amount on the wrong side of an account

44. Many business firms maintain a book of original entry in which all bills to be paid are recorded. 44.____
This book is known as a

A. purchase returns journal
B. subsidiary ledger
C. voucher register
D. notes payable register

45. Many business firms provide a petty cash fund from which to pay for small items in order to avoid the issuing of many small checks. 45.____
If this fund is replenished periodically to restore it to its original amount, the fund is called a(n) ______ fund.

A. imprest
B. debenture
C. adjustment
D. expense reserve

46. A firm which voluntarily terminates business, selling its assets and paying its liabilities, is said to be in 46.____

A. receivership
B. liquidation
C. depletion
D. amortization

47. The phrase *3%-10 days* on an invoice ORDINARILY means that 47.____

A. 3% of the amount must be paid each 10 days
B. the purchaser is entitled to only ten days credit
C. a discount of 3% will be allowed for payment in 10 days
D. the entire amount must be paid in 10 days or a penalty of 3% of the amount due will be added

48. The CHIEF disadvantage of *single-entry* bookkeeping is that it 48.____

A. is too difficult to operate
B. is illegal for income tax purposes
C. provides no possibility of determining net profits
D. furnishes an incomplete picture of the business

49. Sales *minus* cost of goods sold *equals* 49.____

A. net profit
B. gross sales
C. gross profit
D. net sales

50. The amounts of the transactions recorded in a journal are transferred to the general ledger accounts by a process known as 50.____

A. auditing B. balancing C. posting D. verifying

51. A merchant purchased a stock of goods and priced these goods so as to gain 40% on the cost to him. 51.____
If the merchant sold these goods for $840, the COST of these goods to him was

A. $556 B. $600 C. $348 D. $925

52. In the interest at 6% for one full year on a principal sum amounts to $12, the *principal sum* is 52.____

A. $150 B. $96 C. $196 D. $200

53. On October 17, a business man discounted a customer's 90-day non-interest bearing note at his bank. The face of the note was $960, and it was dated September 28. The discount rate was 5%. 53.____
Using a 360-day year, the amount in cash that the business man received from the bank was MOST NEARLY

A. $899.33 B. $950.67 C. $967.50 D. $989.75

54. A certain correctly totaled cash receipts journal contained the following columns: Net Cash Debit, Accounts Receivable, Sales Discounts, and General. 54.____
At the end of April, the totals of the columns were as follows: Net Cash Debit - $18,925.15, Accounts Receivable (not given), Sales Discounts - $379.65, General - $5,639.25.
The TOTAL of the Accounts Receivable column was

A. $11,194.50 B. $21,344.32 C. $7,621.19 D. $13,665.55

55. In its first year of operation, a retail store had cash sales of $49,000 and installment sales of $41,000. 55.____
If 12% of the amount of these installment sales were collected in that year, the TOTAL amount of cash received from sales was

A. $22,176 B. $34,987 C. $53,920 D. $55,650

56. I. Conklin and J. Ulster formed a partnership and agreed to share profits in proportion to their initial capital investments. I. Conklin invested $15,000 and J. Ulster invested $12,500. 56.____
If the profits for the year were $16,500, J. Ulster's share of the profits was

A. $6,750 B. $7,500 C. $8,100 D. $8,300

57. In a certain city, the tax rate on real estate one year was $48.75 per thousand dollars of assessed valuation. If an apartment house in that city was assessed for $185,000, the real estate tax payable by the owner of that house was MOST NEARLY 57.____

A. $9,018.75 B. $9,009.75 C. $8,900.00 D. $8,905.25

58. A correctly totaled cash payments journal contained the following columns: Net Cash, Accounts Payable, Purchase Discounts, General. 58.____
At the end of April, the totals of the columns were as follows: Net Cash - $18,375.60, Accounts Payable - $16,981.19, Purchase Discounts (not given), General - $1,875.37.
The TOTAL of the Purchase Discounts column was

A. $120.36 B. $239.87 C. $480.96 D. $670.51

59. On January 1, the credit balance of the Accounts Payable account in a general ledger was $9,139.87. For the month of January, the Purchase Journal total amounted to $3,467.81; the Accounts Payable column in the Cash Disbursements Journal amounted to $2,935.55; the total of the Returned Purchases Journal for January amounted to $173.15; and the Miscellaneous column in the Cash Disbursements Journal showed that $750 had been paid in January on notes given to creditors and entered in previous months. 59.____
The BALANCE in the Accounts Payable account at the end of January was

A. $8,437.89 B. $9,498.98 C. $9,998.98 D. $10,132.68

60. The bank statement received from his bank by a business man showed a certain balance for the month of June. This bank statement showed a service charge of $5.19 for the month. He discovered that a check drawn by him in the amount of $83.75 and returned by the bank had been entered on the stub of his checkbook as $38.75. He also found that two checks which he had issued, #29 for $37.18 and #33 for $18.69, were not listed on the statement and had not been returned by the bank. The balance in his checkbook before he reconciled it with the balance shown on the bank statement was $8,917.91. 60.____
The BALANCE on the bank statement was

A. $8,903.97 B. $8,923.59 C. $8,997.65 D. $9,303.95

KEY (CORRECT ANSWERS)

1. D	16. D	31. E	46. B
2. A	17. D	32. C	47. C
3. B	18. C	33. A	48. D
4. D	19. D	34. C	49. C
5. D	20. D	35. E	50. C
6. A	21. D	36. B	51. B
7. D	22. C	37. A	52. D
8. A	23. C	38. E	53. B
9. B	24. C	39. B	54. D
10. B	25. C	40. A	55. C
11. C	26. D	41. A	56. B
12. D	27. D	42. D	57. A
13. C	28. A	43. B	58. C
14. D	29. D	44. C	59. B
15. C	30. B	45. A	60. B

TEST 2

Questions 1-25.

DIRECTIONS:
1. Below you will find the general ledger balances on February 28 in the books of C. Dutton.
2. On the following pages, you will find all the entries on the books of C. Dutton for the month of March.
3. In the appropriate spaces on the right, you are to supply the new balances for the accounts called for at the end of March.

The correct balances in the general ledger of C. Dutton on February 28 were as follows: (NOTE: The accounts below have not been arranged in the customary trial balance form.)

Cash	$4,336
Accounts Receivable	8,165
Notes Receivable	2,200
Furniture and Fixtures	9,000
Merchandise Inventory 1/1	4,175
Accounts Payable	5,560
Notes Payable	1,500
Reserve for Depreciation of Furniture and Fixtures	1,800
C. Dutton, Capital	14,162
C. Dutton, Drawing	900
Purchases	42,600
Freight In	36
Rent	1,750
Light	126
Telephone	63
Salaries	4,076
Shipping Expenses	368
Sales	53,200
Sales Biscount	637
Purchase Biscount	596
City Sales Tax Collected	804
Social Security Taxes Payable	96
Withholding Taxes Payable	714

CASH RECEIPTS

Date	Name	Net Cash	Accounts Receivable	Sales Disc.	Miscellaneous Acct.	Miscellaneous Amount
3/1	T. Blint	6,027.00	6,150.00	123.00		
	K . Crowe	1,015.00			Notes Rec.	1,000.00
					Int. Income	15.00
3/10	N. Tandy	3,969.00	4,050.00	81.00		
3/17	Rebuilt Desk Co.	45.00			Furn. & Fixt.	45.00
3/24	J. Walter	2,910.00	3,000.00	90.00		
3/31	National Federal Bank	3,000.00			Notes Payable	3,000.00
		16,966.00	13,200.00	294.00		4,060.00

CASH DISBURSEMENTS

Date		Net Cash	Accts. Pay.	Purch. Disc.	Soc. Sec. Tax	With-hold Tax	Miscellaneous Acct.	Miscellaneous Amount
3/1	Bliss Realty Co.	875.00					Rent	875.00
3/4	Con. Edison	54.00					Light	54.00
3/10	D. LaRue	2,891.00	2,950.00	59.00				
3/15	Payroll	747.00			26.00	175.	Sal.	948.00
3/19	Rebuilt Desk Co.	115.00					Furn/Fixt	115.00
3/26	Jiggs & Co.	3,686.00	3,800.00	114.00				
3/30	Nat'l Fed Bank	1,218.00					Notes Pay.	1200.00
							Int. Cost	18.00
3/31	Payroll	733.00			22.00	171.	Salary	926.00
3/31	C. Dutton	600.00					Draw	600.00
		10,919.00	6,750.00	173.00	48.00	346.00		4736.00

SALES BOOK

Date	Name	Accts. Rec.	Sales	City Sales Tax
3/3	K. Crowe	6,850.00	6,665.00	185.00
3/10	J. Walters	5,730.00	5,730.00	
3/16	N. Tandy	3,100.00	3,007.00	93.00
3/25	Willis & Co.	7,278.00	7,069.00	209.00
3/30	V. Clyburne	2,190.00	2,190.00	
		25,148.00	24,661.00	487.00

PURCHASE BOOK

Date		Accts. Pay.	Purchases	Freight In	Miscellaneous Acct.	Miscellaneous Amount
3/4	Jiggs & Co.	5,212.00	5,070.00	142.00		
3/11	Barton & Co.	320.00			Ins. Prepd.	320.00
3/16	A. Field	6,368.00	6,179.00	189.00		
3/19	Smith Delivery	22.00			Ship. Exp.	22.00
3/23	N.Y. Telephone	29.00			Telephone	29.00
3/26	D. LaRue	3,000.00	3,000.00			
3/29	App & App	7,531.00	7,168.00	363.00		
		22,482.00	21,417.00	694.00		371.00

Supply the balances of the following accounts on March 31 after all posting has been done for March. Put answers in the appropriate spaces on the right. Give amounts only.

1. Cash 1.____
2. Accounts Receivable 2.____
3. Notes Receivable 3.____
4. Insurance Prepaid 4.____
5. Furniture and Fixtures 5.____
6. Accounts Payable 6.____
7. Notes Payable 7.____

8. Reserve for Depreciation of Furniture and Fixtures 8.____

9. C. Dutton, Capital 9.____

10. C. Dutton, Drawing 10.____

11. Purchases 11.____

12. Freight In 12.____

13. Rent 13.____

14. Light 14.____

15. Telephone 15.____

16. Salaries 16.____

17. Shipping Expenses 17.____

18. Sales 18.____

19. Sales Discount 19.____

20. Purchase Discount 20.____

21. City Sales Tax Collected 21.____

22. Social Security Taxes Payable 22.____

23. Withholding Taxes Payable 23.____

24. Interest Income 24.____

25. Interest Cost 25.____

Questions 26-35.

DIRECTIONS: Mr. Adams has a complete set of books - Cash Journals, Purchase and Sales Journals, and a General Journal. Below you will find the General Journal used by Mr. Adams. Under the heading of each money column, you will find a letter of the alphabet. Following the General Journal, there is a series of transactions. You are to determine the correct entry for each transaction and then show on the right in the appropriate space the columns to be used. For example, if a certain transaction results in an entry of $100 in the Notes Receiving Column (on the left side) and an entry of $100 in the General Ledger Column (on the right side), in the appropriate space on the right, you should write A, D. If the record of the transaction requires the use of more than two columns, your answer should contain more than two letters. DO NOT PUT THE AMOUNTS IN YOUR ANSWER SPACE. The LETTERS of the columns to be used are sufficient. If a transaction requires no entry in the General Journal, write *None* in the appropriate space in your answer space, even though a record would be made in some other journal.

GENERAL JOURNAL

Notes Receivable	Accounts Payable	General Ledger	L. F.		General Ledger	Accounts Receivable	Notes Payable
A	B	C			D	E	F

26. We sent Tripp & Co. a 30-day trade acceptance for $500 for merchandise sold him today. They accepted it. 26.____

27. The proprietor, Mr. Adams, returned $100 in cash to be deposited, representing Traveling Expenses he had not used. 27.____

28. An entry in the purchase journal last month for a purchase invoice from V. Valides for $647 was erroneously entered in the purchase journal as $746 and posted as such. 28.____

29. A check for $200 received from Mr. Breen was erroneously credited to account of P. Ungar. 29.____

30. In posting the totals of the cash receipts journal last month, an item of bank discount of $30 on our note for $1500 discounted for 60 days was included in the total posted to the sales discount account. 30.____

31. M. Hogan paid his note of $600 and interest of $12 and his account was credited for $612. 31.____

32. Mr. Blow informed us he could not pay his invoice of $2000 due today. Instead, he sent us his 30-day note for $2000 for 30 days bearing interest at 6% per annum. 32.____

33. The proprietor, Mr. Adams, drew $75 to buy his daughter a U.S. Bond. 33.____

34. Mr. O'Brien wrote to us that we overcharged him on an invoice last week. 34.____

35. Returned $120 worth of merchandise to Pecora & Co. and received their credit memorandum. 35.____

Questions 36-50.

DIRECTIONS: In Questions 36 to 50, you will find a list of accounts with a number before each.

1. Cash
2. Accounts Receivable
3. Notes Receivable
4. Notes Receivable Discounted
5. Furniture and Fixtures
6. Delivery Equipment
7. Insurance Prepaid
8. Depreciation on Delivery Equipment
9. Bad Debts
10. Purchases
11. Discount on Purchases
12. Sales
13. Discount on Sales
14. Accounts Payable
15. Notes Payable
16. Interest Cost
17. Reserve for Depreciation on Delivery Equipment
18. Reserve for Bad Debts
19. Sales Taxes Collected
20. Ben Miller, Capital
21. Ben Miller, Drawing
22. Interest Income
23. Purchase Returns

Using the number in front of each account title (using no accounts not listed), make journal entries for the transactions given below. Do not write the names of the accounts in your answer space. Simply indicate in the proper space on the right the numbers of the accounts to be debited or credited. Always give the number or numbers of the accounts to be debited first, then give the number or numbers of accounts to be credited. For example, if furniture and fixtures and delivery equipment are to be debited, and cash and notes payable are to be credited in a certain transaction, then write in your answer space 5, 6 - 1, 15 (use a dash to separate the debits from the credits).

36. F. Pierce, a customer, went into bankruptcy owing us $600. We received a check for $200. 36.____

37. Later in the month, we are informed that there is no possibility of collecting the balance from F. Pierce. There is a sufficient balance in the Reserve for Bad Debts to take care of the above. 37.____

38. Set up the Depreciation on the Delivery Equipment for the year amounting to $240. 38.____

39. Discounted M. Colby's note for $500 today and received $490 in proceeds. 39.____

40. Mr. Miller, the proprietor, invested $2000 in the business. 40.____

41. Paid our note due to Dillon & Co. today for $800 with interest of $16. 41.____

42. Accepted Finnegan's trade acceptance for $1500 for merchandise bought today. 42.____

43. Create a Reserve for Bad Debts of $2000 at the end of the year. 43.____

44. Returned to Dillon & Co. $30 worth of damaged merchandise for credit. They allowed it. 44.____

45. G. Garry claimed a discount of $12 which we had failed to allow him. He had already paid his bill. Sent him check for $12. 45.____

46. On one sale during the month, we had failed to collect the Sales Tax of $15. Wrote to the customer and he sent us a check for $15. 46.____

47. M. Colby paid his note due today which we had discounted two months ago. 47.____

48. Bought a new safe for $875 from Cramer & Co., terms 2/10, n/60 days. Agreed to pay them in 60 days. 48.____

49. Bought merchandise during the month amounting to $17,500 - all on account. 49.____

50. On December 31, paid for a Fire Insurance policy to run for three years from that date - premium was $480. 50.____

51. The following information was taken from the ledger of Peter Dolan on Dec. 31 after adjusting entries had been posted to the ledger. 51.____

Sales Income	$60,000
Sales Returns	3,500
Mdse. Purchases	42,000
Inventory of 1/1	9,400
Sales Taxes Payable	360
Freight Inward	225
Inventory 12/31	7,640
Insurance Unexpired	163

Find the gross profit on Sales for the year.

52. On March 31, your bank sent you a statement of account. You compared the canceled checks with the stubs in your checkbook and found the following: 52.___

Check #34 - $56.00 had not been paid by the bank
#44 - $38.00 had been paid by the bank as $38.89 because the amount on the check did not agree with your stub in the checkbook
#52 - $76.50 had not been returned by the bank, though the check had been certified
#57 - $127.42 had not been paid by the bank

What total amount would you deduct from the balance on the bank's statement as checks outstanding?

53. On April 30, Mr. Jolley received his statement of account from the bank. A comparison of the bank statement and your checkbook revealed the following: Checkbook balance $5,640; this included a deposit of $325 on the last day of April which had not been entered on the bank statement. 53.___

You also find the following:

Check #69 - $89.00 had not been paid by the bank
#70 - Paid by the bank as $47.55, had been entered in your checkbook as $45.57
#76 - $114.30 had not been paid by the bank

The bank statement included a debit memo of $4.00 for excessive activity during the month.

What was the balance on the bank statement?

54. An invoice dated January 15 for merchandise you bought added up to $876.00. The terms were 3/10, n/60, F.O.B. DESTINATION. When the goods arrived, you paid freight amounting to $8.50. On January 20, you returned goods billed at $26 and received credit therefor. You paid the bill on January 24. 54.___

What was the amount of your check?

55. Income taxes paid by residents of a certain state are based on the balance of taxable income at the following 55.___

rates: 2% on first $1000 or less
3% on 2nd and 3rd $1000
4% on 4th and 5th $1000
5% on 6th and 7th $1000
6% on 8th and 9th $1000
7% on all over $9000

What would be the NORMAL income tax to be paid by a resident of that state whose taxable balance of income was $6,750?

56. A salesman's gross earnings for the year came to $8,820. His rate of Commission was 5% of his sales to customers after deducting returns by customers. During the year, his customers returned 10% of the goods they purchased. What were his total sales during the year before deducting returns? 56.___

57. On December 31, the insurance account contained a debit for $144 for a three-year fire insurance policy dated August 1. What amount should be listed on the balance sheet of December 31 of that year? 57.___

58. A partnership began business on January 1 with partners' investments of $26,000. During the year, the partners drew $18,500 for personal use. On December 31, the assets of the firm were $46,300, and the liabilities were $15,600. What was the firm's net profit for the year? (Write P or L before your answer.) 58.____

59. The rent income account of a real estate firm showed a total balance of $75,640 at the end of 1986. Of this amount, $3,545 represented prepaid 1987 rents. The account also included entries for 1986 rents due from tenants but not yet collected, amounting to $2,400.
What amount should be listed on the profit and loss statement as rent income for 1986? 59.____

60. You discounted a customer's note for $7,200 at your bank at the rate of 6% and received net proceeds of $7,182.
How many days did the note have to run from date of discount to date of maturity? (Use 360 days to the year.) 60.____

Questions 61-90.

DIRECTIONS: In Questions 61 to 90, you will find a list of ledger accounts. Indicate whether an account is generally listed in the Trial Balance as a DEBIT or as a CREDIT by putting the letter *D* or the letter *C* in the correct space on the right for each account listed.

61. Sales 61.____

62. Land 62.____

63. Notes Payable 63.____

64. Traveling Expenses 64.____

65. Purchases 65.____

66. Buildings 66.____

67. Merchandise Inventory 67.____

68. Machinery and Equipment 68.____

69. Notes Receivable 69.____

70. Bonds Payable 70.____

71. Advertising 71.____

72. Delivery Expense 72.____

73. Cash 73.____

74. Accounts Payable 74.____
75. Interest on Bonds 75.____
76. Real Estate Taxes 76.____
77. Accounts Receivable 77.____
78. Don Burch, Proprietor 78.____
79. Sales Discount 79.____
80. Withholding Taxes 80.____
81. Depreciation 81.____
82. Prepaid Insurance 82.____
83. Reserve for Dep. on Buildings 83.____
84. Rent Income 84.____
85. Reserve for Bad Debts 85.____
86. Don Burch, Drawing Account 86.____
87. Sales Returns 87.____
88. Bad Debts 88.____
89. Purchase Discount 89.____
90. Reserve for Dep. on Machinery & Equipment 90.____

KEY (CORRECT ANSWERS)

1.	$ 10,383	31.	C,D,D	61.	C
2.	$ 20,113	32.	A,E	62.	D
3.	$ 1,200	33.	None	63.	C
4.	$ 320	34.	C,E	64.	D
5.	$ 9,070	35.	B,D	65.	D
6.	$ 21,292	36.	1-2	66.	D
7.	$ 3,300	37.	18-2	67.	D
8.	$ 1,800	38.	8-17	68.	D
9.	$ 14,162	39.	1,16-4	69.	D
10.	$ 1,500	40.	1-20	70.	C
11.	$ 64,017	41.	15,16-1	71.	D
12.	$ 730	42.	14-15	72.	D
13.	$ 2,625	43.	9-18	73.	D
14.	$ 180	44.	14-23	74.	C
15.	$ 92	45.	13-1	75.	D
16.	$ 5,950	46.	1-19	76.	D
17.	$ 390	47.	4-3	77.	D
18.	$ 77,861	48.	5-14	78.	C
19.	$ 931	49.	10-14	79.	D
20.	$ 769	50.	7-1	80.	C
21.	$1,291	51.	$12,515	81.	D
22.	$ 144	52.	$ 183.42	82.	D
23.	$1,060	53.	$ 5,512.32	83.	C
24.	$ 15	54.	$ 816	84.	C
25.	$ 18	55.	$ 247.50	85.	C
26.	A-E	56.	$196,000	86.	D
27.	None	57.	$ 124	87.	D
28.	B-D	58.	P $23,200	88.	D
29.	C,E	59.	$72,095	89.	C
30.	C,D	60.	15	90.	C

TEST 3

DIRECTIONS: Each question or incomplete statement is followed by several suggested answers or completions. Select the one that BEST answers the question or completes the statement. *PRINT THE LETTER OF THE CORRECT ANSWER IN THE SPACE AT THE RIGHT.*

1. Of the following taxes, the one which is levied MOST NEARLY in accordance with ability to pay is a(n) ______ tax. 1.____

   A. excise
   B. income
   C. general property
   D. sales

2. When a check has been lost, the bank on which it is drawn should ORDINARILY be notified and instructed to 2.____

   A. stop payment on the check
   B. issue a duplicate of the check
   C. charge the account of the drawer for the amount of the check
   D. certify the check

3. The profit and loss statement prepared for a retail store does NOT ordinarily show 3.____

   A. the cost of goods sold
   B. depreciation of fixtures and equipment
   C. expenditures for salaries of employees
   D. the net worth of the proprietor

4. When two business corporations join their assets and liabilities to form a new corporation, the procedures is called a(n) 4.____

   A. merger
   B. liquidation
   C. receivership
   D. exchange

5. The method of depreciation which deducts an equal amount each full year of an asset's life is called ______ depreciation. 5.____

   A. sum-of-years digits
   B. declining balance
   C. straight-line
   D. service-hours

6. A fixed asset is an asset that 6.____

   A. is held primarily for sale to customers
   B. is used in the conduct of the business until worn out or replaced
   C. is readily convertible into cash
   D. has no definite value

7. The gross profit on sales for a period is determined by 7.____

   A. subtracting the cost of goods sold from the sales
   B. subtracting the sales returns and the discounts on sales from the gross sales
   C. subtracting the sales from the purchases for the period
   D. finding the difference between the inventory of merchandise at the beginning of the period and the inventory of merchandise at the end of the period

8. The term *auditing* refers to the 8.____

A. entering of amounts from the journals into the general ledger
B. reconciliation of the accounts in a subsidiary ledger with the controlling account in the general ledger
C. preparation of a trial balance of the accounts in the general ledger
D. examination of the general ledger and other records of a concern to determine its true financial condition

9. A voucher register is a 9.____

A. type of electric cash register
B. list of customers whose accounts are past due
C. list of the assets of a business
D. book in which bills to be paid are recorded

10. The account DISCOUNT ON PURCHASES is *properly* closed directly to the ______ account. 10.____

A. Accounts Payable
B. Sales
C. Purchases
D. Fixtures

11. The account UNEARNED RENTAL INCOME is *usually* considered a(n) ______ account. 11.____

A. asset
B. nominal
C. capital
D. liability

12. A controlling account is an account which contains 12.____

A. the totals of *all* the expense accounts in the general ledger
B. the total of the amounts entered in the accounts in a subsidiary ledger
C. the total of the depreciation on fixtures claimed in *all* preceding years
D. *all* totals of the income and expense accounts before closing to the Profit and Loss account

13. The purpose of the DRAWING account in the general ledger of an individual enterprise is to show the 13.____

A. salaries paid to the employees
B. amounts paid to independent contractors for services rendered
C. amounts taken by the proprietor for his personal use
D. total of payments made for general expenses of the business

14. The phrase *2%/10 net 30 days* on an invoice ORDINARILY means that 14.____

A. 2% of the amount must be paid within 30 days
B. the purchaser must add 2% to the amount of the invoice if he fails to pay within 30 days
C. the entire amount must be paid within 30 days
D. the purchaser may deduct 2% from the amount if he pays within 30 days

15. The ESSENTIAL characteristic of a C.O.D. sale of merchandise is that the 15.____

A. purchaser pays for the merchandise upon its receipt by him
B. seller guarantees the merchandise to be as specified by him
C. merchandise is delivered by a common carrier
D. purchaser is permitted to pay for the merchandise in convenient installments

16. If the drawer of a check makes an error in writing the amount of the check, he should 16.____

A. erase the error and insert the correct amount
B. cross out the error and insert the correct amount
C. destroy the check and prepare another one
D. write the correct amount directly above the incorrect one

17. States do NOT levy a(n) ______ tax. 17.____

A. unemployment insurance
B. income
C. corporation franchise
D. export

18. The cost of goods sold by a retail store is PROPERLY determined by 18.____

A. *adding* the closing inventory to the total of the opening inventory and the purchases for the year
B. *deducting* the closing inventory from the total of the opening inventory and the purchases for the year
C. *deducting* the total of the opening and closing inventories from the purchases for the year
D. *adding* the total of the opening and closing inventories

19. The PRIMARY purpose of a trial balance is to determine 19.____

A. that all transactions have been entered in the journals
B. the accuracy of the totals in the general ledger
C. the correctness of the amounts entered in the journals
D. that amounts have been posted to the proper accounts in the general ledger

20. The SURPLUS account of a corporation is *ordinarily* used to record 20.____

A. the actual amount subscribed by stockholders
B. the amount of profits earned by the corporation
C. any excess of current assets over current liabilities
D. the total of the fixed assets of the corporation

Questions 21-30.

DIRECTIONS: Each of Questions 21 to 30 consists of a typical transaction of Our Business followed by the debit and credit (amounts omitted) of the journal entry for that transaction. For each of these questions, the debit and credit given may be appropriately classified under one of the following categories:

A. The debit of the journal entry is CORRECT but the credit is INCORRECT.
B. The debit of the journal entry is INCORRECT but the credit is CORRECT.
C. BOTH the debit and the credit of the journal entry are correct.
D. BOTH the debit and the credit of the journal entry are incorrect.

Examine each question carefully. Then, in the correspondingly numbered space on the right, mark as your answer the letter preceding the category which is the BEST of the four suggested above.

SAMPLE QUESTION: We purchased a desk for cash.
Debit: Office Equipment
Credit: Accounts Payable

In this example, the debit is correct but the credit is incorrect. Therefore, you should mark A as your answer.

21. We sent a check for $500 to R. Thomas in payment for an invoice for that amount. 21.____
Debit: Cash Credit: Accounts Receivable

22. We took merchandise, amounting to $35, for our own use. 22.____
Debit: Proprietor, Personal Credit: Purchases

23. Arthur Townsend's 90-day note for $350, which was discounted by us at our bank last month, was paid by him today. 23.____
Debit: Notes Receivable Discounted
Credit: Accounts Receivable

24. We sold merchandise to T. Wilson on account of $275. 24.____
Debit: Accounts Payable Credit: Sales

25. We returned damaged merchandise to B. Lowell and received a credit memorandum from him for $28. 25.____
Debit: Accounts Payable
Credit: Sales Returns and Allowances

26. We paid our 30-day note given to Mr. Kane for $650 without interest. 26.____
Debit: Notes Receivable Credit: Cash

27. We sent Chet Carr a check for $10.50 for a discount he had forgotten to take when he paid us for merchandise this week. 27.____
Debit: Sales Discounts Credit: Cash

28. The bank loaned us $1000, and we invested it in the business. 28.____
Debit: Cash Credit: Loan Receivable

29. We recorded depreciation for the year on our office equipment. 29.____
Debit: Reserve for Depreciation of Office Equipment
Credit: Depreciation of Office Equipment

30. One of our customers, Allen Koren, was declared bankrupt and his debt of $25 to us was canceled. 30.____
Debit: Reserve for Bad Debts Credit: Accounts Receivable

Questions 31-45.

DIRECTIONS: Questions 31 to 45 consist of a list of some of the accounts in the general ledger of a corporation which operates a retail store. Indicate whether each account listed contains generally a debit or credit balance by marking the letter D (for debit balance) or the letter C (for credit balance) in the correspondingly numbered space on the right.
For example, for the account Cash, which generally contains a debit balance, you would mark the letter D as your answer.

31. Rent Expense 31.___

32. Allowance for Depreciation of Fixtures 32.___

33. Sales Returns and Allowances 33.___

34. Security Deposit for Electricity 34.___

35. Accrued Salaries Payable 35.___

36. Dividends Payable 36.___

37. Petty Cash Fund 37.___

38. Notes Receivable Discounted 38.___

39. Surplus 39.___

40. Capital Stock Authorized 40.___

41. Insurance Expense 41.___

42. Sales for Cash 42.___

43. Purchase Discounts 43.___

44. Automobile Delivery Equipment 44.___

45. Bad Debts Expense 45.___

Questions 46-60.

DIRECTIONS: Questions 46 to 60 consist of a list of some of the accounts in a general ledger. For the purpose of preparing financial statements, each of these accounts is to be classified into one of the following five major classifications, lettered A to E, as follows:
A. Assets B. Liabilities C. Income D. Expense E. Capital You are to indicate the classification to which each belongs by marking the appropriate letter, A, B, C, D or E. in the correspondingly numbered space on the right. For example, for the account MERCHANDISE INVENTORY, which is an asset account, you would mark the letter A as your answer.

46. Purchases 46.___

47. Prepaid Interest 47.___

48. Cash in Bank 48.___

49. Depreciation of Fixtures 49.___

50. Accounts Receivable 50.____

51. Mortgage Payable 51.____

52. Accrued Interest Receivable 52.____

53. Bad Debts 53.____

54. Insurance Expired 54.____

55. Treasury Stock 55.____

56. Investments 56.____

57. Loan to Partner 57.____

58. Unearned Rent Received 58.____

59. Petty Cash Fund 59.____

60. Loss on Sale of Equipment 60.____

KEY (CORRECT ANSWERS)

1. B	16. C	31. D	46. D
2. A	17. D	32. C	47. A
3. D	18. B	33. D	48. A
4. A	19. B	34. D	49. D
5. C	20. B	35. C	50. A
6. B	21. D	36. C	51. B
7. A	22. C	37. D	52. A
8. D	23. A	38. C	53. D
9. D	24. B	39. C	54. D
10. C	25. A	40. C	55. E
11. D	26. B	41. D	56. A
12. B	27. C	42. C	57. A
13. C	28. A	43. C	58. B
14. C	29. D	44. D	59. A
15. A	30. C	45. D	60. D

EXAMINATION SECTION
TEST 1

DIRECTIONS: Each question or incomplete statement is followed by several suggested answers or completions. Select the one that BEST answers the question or completes the statement. *PRINT THE LETTER OF THE CORRECT ANSWER IN THE SPACE AT THE RIGHT.*

Questions 1-5.

DIRECTIONS: Questions 1 through 5 are to be answered on the basis of the statement account shown below.

STATEMENT OF ACCOUNT

Regal Tools, Inc.
136 Culver Street
Cranston, R.I. 02910

TO: Vista, Inc.
572 No. Copeland Ave.
Pawtucket, R.I. 02800

DATE: March 31

DATE	ITEM	CHARGES	PAYMENTS AND CREDITS	BALANCE
	Previous Balance			785.35
March 8	Payment		785.35	----
12	Invoice 17-582	550 --		550.00
17	Invoice 17-692	700 --		1250.00
31	Payment		550.00	700.00

PAY LAST AMOUNT SHOWN IN BALANCE COLUMN

1. Which company is the customer? 1.____

2. What total amount was charged by the customer during March? 2.____

3. How much does the customer owe on March 31? 3.____

4. On which accounting schedule would Vista list Regal? 4.____

5. The terms on invoice 17-582 were 3/20, n/45. 5.____
   What was the CORRECT amount for which the check should have been written when payment was made?

6. Which item is NOT a source document? 6.___
A(n)

A. invoice
B. magnetic tape
C. punched card
D. telephone conversation

7. What is double-entry accounting? 7.___

A. Journalizing and posting
B. Recording debit and credit parts for a transaction
C. Using carbon paper when preparing a source document
D. Posting a debit or credit and computing the new account balance

8. The balance in the asset account Supplies is $600. An ending inventory shows $200 of supplies on hand. 8.___
The adjusting entry should be

A. debit Supplies Expense for $200, credit Supplies for $200
B. credit Supplies Expense for $200, debit Supplies for $200
C. debit Supplies Expense for $400, credit Supplies for $400
D. credit Supplies Expense for $400, debit Supplies for $400

9. What is the purpose of preparing an Income Statement? 9.___
To

A. report the net income or net loss
B. show the owner's claims against the assets
C. prove that the accounting equation is in balance
D. prove that the total debits equal the total credits

10. Which account does NOT belong on the Income Statement? 10.___

A. Salaries Payable
B. Rental Revenue
C. Advertising Expense
D. Sales Returns and Allowances

11. The source document for entries made in a Purchases Journal is a purchase 11.___

A. order B. requisition C. invoice D. register

12. A business check guaranteed for payment by the bank is called a 12.___

A. bank draft
B. certified check
C. cashier's check
D. personal check

13. The entry that closes the Purchases Account contains a 13.___

A. debit to Purchases
B. debit to Purchases Returns and Allowances
C. credit to Purchases
D. credit to Income and Expense Summary

14. Which account would NOT appear on a Balance Sheet? 14.____

A. Office Equipment
B. Transportation In
C. Mortgage Payable
D. Supplies on Hand

15. Which entry is made at the end of the fiscal period for the purpose of updating the Prepaid Insurance Account? 15.____
_______ entry.

A. Correcting
B. Closing
C. Adjusting
D. Reversing

16. Which deduction from gross pay is NOT required by law? 16.____

A. Hospitalization insurance
B. FICA tax
C. Federal income tax
D. New York State income tax

17. What is the last date on which a 2 percent cash discount can be taken for an invoice dated October 15 with terms of 2/10, n/30? 17.____

A. October 15
B. October 17
C. October 25
D. November 14

18. Which item on the bank reconciliation statement would require the business to record a journal entry? 18.____
A(n)

A. deposit in transit
B. outstanding check
C. canceled check
D. bank service charge

19. Which is NOT an essential component of a computer? 19.____
A(n)

A. input device
B. central processor
C. output device
D. telecommunicator

20. Which group of accounts could appear on a post-closing trial balance? 20.____

A. Petty Cash; Accounts Receivable; FICA Taxes Payable
B. Office Furniture; Office Expense; Supplies on Hand
C. Supplies Expense; Sales; Advertising Expense
D. Sales Discount; Rent Expense; J. Smith, Drawing

21. The withdrawals of cash by the owner are recorded in the owner's drawing account as a(n) 21.____

A. adjusting entry
B. closing entry
C. credit
D. debit

22. An account in the General Ledger which shows a total of a related Subsidiary Ledger is referred to as a(n) _______ account. 22.____

A. revenue
B. controlling
C. temporary
D. owner's equity

23. 23. ____

Which type of endorsement is shown above?

A. Restrictive
B. Blank
C. Full
D. Qualified

24. Which is a chronological record of all the transactions of a business? 24. ____

A. Worksheet
B. Income Statement
C. Journal
D. Trial balance

25. Which error would NOT be revealed by the preparation of a trial balance? 25. ____

A. Posting of an entire transaction more than once
B. Incorrectly pencil footing the balance of a general ledger account
C. Posting a debit of $320 as $230
D. Omitting an account with a balance

26. The Cash Receipts Journal is used to record the 26. ____

A. purchase of merchandise for cash
B. purchase of merchandise on credit
C. sale of merchandise for cash
D. sale of merchandise on credit

27. On a systems flowchart, which symbol is commonly used to indicate the direction of the flow of work? 27. ____
A(n)

A. arrow
B. circle
C. diamond
D. rectangle

28. Which account balance would be eliminated by a closing entry at the end of the fiscal period? 28. ____

A. Office Equipment
B. Owner's Drawing
C. Owner's Capital
D. Mortgage Payable

29. In a data processing system, the handling and manipulation of data according to precise procedures is called 29. ____

A. input
B. processing
C. storage
D. output

30. Which financial statement reflects the cumulative financial position of the business? 30. ____

A. Bank statement
B. Income statement
C. Trial balance
D. Balance sheet

31. Which account should be credited when recording a cash proof showing an overage? 31.____

A. Sales
B. Cash
C. Cash Short and Over
D. Sales Returns and Allowances

32. In which section of the income statement would the purchases account be shown? 32.____

A. Cost of Goods Sold
B. Income from Sales
C. Operating Expenses
D. Other Expenses

33. What is an invoice? 33.____
A(n)

A. order for the shipment of goods
B. order for the purchase of goods
C. receipt for goods purchased
D. statement listing goods purchased

34. A business uses a Sales Journal, a Purchases Journal, a Cash Receipts Journal, a Cash Payments Journal, and a General Journal. 34.____
In which journal would a credit memorandum received from a creditor be recorded?
_______ Journal

A. Sales
B. Purchases
C. General
D. Cash Receipts

35. Which account is debited to record a weekly payroll? 35.____

A. Employees Income Tax Payable
B. FICA Taxes Payable
C. General Expense
D. Salaries Expense

KEY (CORRECT ANSWERS)

1. Vista, Inc.
2. $1,250
3. $700
4. Accts. Payable
5. $533.50
6. D
7. B
8. C
9. A
10. A
11. C
12. B
13. C
14. D
15. C
16. A
17. C
18. D
19. D
20. A
21. D
22. B
23. A
24. C
25. A
26. C
27. A
28. B
29. B
30. D
31. C
32. A
33. D
34. C
35. D

EXAMINATION SECTION

TEST 1

DIRECTIONS: Each question or incomplete statement is followed by several suggested answers or completions. Select the one that BEST answers the question or completes the statement. *PRINT THE LETTER OF THE CORRECT ANSWER IN THE SPACE AT THE RIGHT.*

1. The owner's equity in a business may derive from which of the following sources? 1.______
   I. Excess of revenue over expenses
   II. Investment by the owner
   III. Accounts payable

   A. I only
   B. II only
   C. III only
   D. I and II
   E. I, II and III

2. Entries made on the books at the end of a period to take care of changes occurring in accounts are called ______ entries. 2.______
   A. fiscal
   B. closing
   C. reversing
   D. correcting
   E. adjusting

3. In accounting, net income should be defined as an increase in 3.______
   A. assets
   B. cash
   C. merchandise
   D. sales
   E. capital

4. Treasury stock is CORRECTLY defined as 4.______
   A. a corporation's own stock that has been issued and then reacquired
   B. new issues of a corporation's stock before they are sold on the open market
   C. stock issued by the United States Office of the Treasury
   D. any stock that a corporation acquires and holds for more than 90 days
   E. any stock held by a corporation that receives dividends in excess of 5 percent of initial cost of the stock

5. The Accumulated Depreciation account should be shown in the financial statements as 5.____
    A. an operating expense
    B. an extraordinary loss
    C. a liability
    D. stockholders' equity
    E. a contra (deduction) to an asset account

6. If fixed expenses are $26,000 and variable expenses are 75 percent of sales, the net income that would result from $500,000 in sales is 6.____
    A. $75,000
    B. $99,000
    C. $200,000
    D. $375,000
    E. $401,000

7. Cost of goods sold is determined by which of the following? 7.____
    A. Beginning inventory plus net purchases minus ending inventory
    B. Beginning inventory plus purchases plus purchase returns minus ending inventory
    C. Beginning inventory minus net purchases plus ending inventory
    D. Purchases minus transportation-in plus beginning inventory minus ending inventory
    E. Net sales minus ending inventory

8. Company X produces chairs of a single type, it has a plant capacity of 50,000 chairs per year and total fixed expenses of $100,000 per year. Variable costs per chair are $2.00 and the current selling price is $5.00 per chair. At the beginning of 2016, the company purchases a specialized machine that costs $10,000, lasts one year, and reduces variable costs to $1.50 per chair. If the company produces and sells at 90 percent of capacity, what is the net income for 2016? 8.____
    A. $8,750
    B. $23,000
    C. $47,500
    D. $50,000
    E. $83,000

9. All of the following T-accounts contain the correct sides that would be used for increasing and decreasing an account EXCEPT 9.____

A.

Revenue	
Decrease	Increase

B.

Assets	
Increase	Decrease

C.

Expenses	
Increase	Decrease

D.

Owner's Equity	
Increase	Decrease

E.

Liabilities	
Decrease	Increase

10. Green Corporation with assets of $5,000,000 and liabilities of $2,000,000 has 6,000 shares of capital stock outstanding (par value $300). What is the book value per share? 10.______
    A. $200
    B. $300
    C. $500
    D. $833
    E. None of the above

11. Of the following, the BEST description of a controlling account is that it is a 11.______
    A. schedule of accounts payable
    B. purchase form that itemizes merchandise bought
    C. ledger that contains a single type of account
    D. statement that lists the individual account balances in the creditors' ledger
    E. general ledger account that summarizes the balance in the accounts of a subsidiary ledger

12. At the end of the fiscal year, a company estimates that $4,300 of Accounts Receivable will be uncollectible. If, prior to adjustment, the company's Allowance for Bad Debts account has a credit balance of $1,600, what is the APPROPRIATE adjusting entry? 12.______

	Debit	Credit	Amount
A.	Allowance for Bad Debts	Bad Debts Expense	$4,300
B.	Allowance for Bad Debts	Accounts Receivable	$4,300
C.	Accounts Receivable	Allowance for Bad Debts	$1,600
D.	Bad Debts Expense	Allowance for Bad Debts	$2,700
E.	Bad Debts Expense	Accounts Receivable	$2,700

13. A fast-moving widget stamping machine was purchased for cash. The list price was $4,000 with an applicable trade discount of 20 percent and a cash discount allowable of 2/10, n/30. Payment was made within the discount period. Freight costs of $100, F.O.B. origin, were paid. In order to install the machine properly, a platform was built and wiring installed for a total cost of $200. The trial run costs were $300 for labor and $50 for materials. The cost of the machine would be recorded as 13.______
    A. $3,626
    B. $3,628
    C. $3,786
    D. $3,828
    E. $4,178

14. All of the following expenditures should be charged to an asset account rather than an expense account of the current period EXCEPT the cost of 14.______
    A. overhauling a delivery truck, which extends its useful life by two years
    B. purchasing a new component for a machine, which serves to increase the machine's productive capacity
    C. constructing a parking lot for a leased building
    D. installing a new piece of equipment
    E. replacing worn-out tires on a delivery truck

15. In a period of rising prices, which of the following inventory methods results in the HIGHEST cost of goods sold? 15.______
    A. FIFO
    B. LIFO
    C. Average cost
    D. Periodic inventory
    E. Perpetual inventory

16. A company forecasts that during the next year it will be able to sell 80,000 units of its special product at a competitive selling price of $10 per unit. The company has the capacity to produce 120,000 units per year. Its total fixed costs are $528,000. Its variable costs are estimated at $3 per unit. The company has the opportunity to sell 10,000 additional units during the same year at a special contract price of $50,000. This special contract will not affect the regular sales volume or price. 16.______
    Acceptance of the contract will cause the year's net income to
    A. increase by $20,000
    B. increase by $26,000
    C. increase by $50,000
    D. decrease by $50,000
    E. decrease by $24,000

17. Which of the following standard cost variances provides information about the extent to which the manufacturing plant of a company was used at normal capacity? 17.______
    A. Materials quantity (usage) variance
    B. Labor efficiency (time) variance
    C. Labor rate variance
    D. Overhead spending (controllable) variance
    E. Overhead volume variance

18. The following information refers to the purchase of merchandise by L Company. List price of merchandise, $1,050; trade discount 20 percent, 2/10, n/30; F.O.B. shipping point; freight cost prepaid by seller and added to the invoice, $100. What is the net amount to be paid to the vendor, within the discount period, for the merchandise? 18.______
    A. $819.00
    B. $901.60
    C. $919.00
    D. $921.20
    E. $923.20

19. X Corporation declares and issues a 5 percent stock dividend on common stock, payable in common stock, shortly after the close of the year. All of the following statements about the nature and effect of the dividend are true EXCEPT: 19.______
    A. total stockholders' equity in the corporation is not changed
    B. dividend does not constitute income to the stockholders
    C. book value per share of common stock is not changed
    D. amount of retained earnings is reduced
    E. amount of total assets is not changed

20. The financial statement prepared to report the financing and investing activities of a business entity for a period of time is called the 20.______
    A. Income Statement
    B. Statement of Retained Earnings
    C. Balance Sheet
    D. Statement of Changes in Owners' Equity
    E. Statement of Changed in Financial Position

21. A feature of the process cost system that is NOT a feature of the job order cost system is 21.______
    A. computation of the equivalent units of production
    B. compilation of the costs of each batch or job produced
    C. use of the Raw Materials Inventory account
    D. preparation of a Cost of Goods Manufactured statement for each accounting period
    E. application of manufacturing overhead on a predetermined basis

22. Net purchases for the year amounted to $80,000. The merchandise inventory at the beginning of the year was $19,000. On sales of $120,000, a 30 percent gross profit on the selling price was realized. The inventory at the end of the year was 22.______
    A. $13,000
    B. $15,000
    C. $17,000
    D. $25,000
    E. $63,000

23. The balance sheet of Harold Company shows current assets of $200,000 and current liabilities of $100,000. The company uses cash to acquire merchandise inventory. As a result of this transaction, which of the following is TRUE of working capital and the current ratio? 23.______
    A. Both are unchanged
    B. Working capital is unchanged; the current ratio increases
    C. Both decrease
    D. Working capital decreases; the current ratio increases
    E. Working capital decreases; the current ratio is unchanged

24. *In determining net income from business operations, the costs involved in generating revenue should be charged against that revenue.* 24.______
    The statement above BEST describes the ______ principle.
    A. cost
    B. going-concern
    C. profit
    D. matching
    E. business entity

25. Which of the following is the BEST explanation of the amount reported on the balance sheet as accumulated depreciation? 25.____
    A. Self-insurance fund to protect against losses of the related assets from fire or other casualty
    B. Decrease in market value of the related assets
    C. Cash accumulated to purchase replacements as the related assets wear out
    D. Cost of the related assets which has been allocated to operations
    E. Estimated amount needed to replace the related assets as they wear out

---

KEY (CORRECT ANSWERS)

1. D	11. E	21. A
2. E	12. D	22. B
3. E	13. C	23. A
4. A	14. E	24. D
5. E	15. B	25. D
6. B	16. A	
7. A	17. E	
8. C	18. E	
9. D	19. C	
10. C	20. E	

TEST 2

DIRECTIONS: Each question or incomplete statement is followed by several suggested answers or completions. Select the one that BEST answers the question or completes the statement. *PRINT THE LETTER OF THE CORRECT ANSWER IN THE SPACE AT THE RIGHT.*

1. What is the number of days' inventory on hand for a firm with cost of goods sold of $750,000 and average ending inventory of $150,000? 1.______
   A. 5
   B. 10
   C. 20
   D. 50
   E. 73

2. During the current year, accounts receivable increased from $27,000 to $41,000, and sales were $225,000. Based on this information, how much cash did the company collect from its customers during the year? 2.______
   A. $211,000
   B. $225,000
   C. $239,000
   D. $252,000
   E. $266,000

3. Accounts receivable turnover helps determine 3.______
   A. the balance of accounts payable
   B. customers who have recently paid their bills
   C. how quickly a firm collects cash on its credit sales
   D. when to write off delinquent accounts
   E. credit sales

4. The income statement is designed to measure 4.______
   A. whether a firm is able to pay its bills
   B. how solvent a company has been
   C. how much cash flow a firm is likely to generate
   D. the financial position of a firm
   E. the results of business operations

5. A company prepares a bank reconciliation in order to 5.______
   A. determine the correct amount of the cash balance
   B. satisfy banking regulations
   C. determine deposits not yet recorded by the bank
   D. double-check the amount of petty cash
   E. record all check disbursements

6. An inventory valuation method usually affects 6.______
   A. the cost of goods sold but not the balance sheet
   B. the balance sheet but not the cost of goods sold
   C. both the income statement and the balance sheet
   D. neither the income statement nor the balance sheet
   E. the cost of goods sold, but not the income statement

7. A liability for dividends is recorded on the ________ date. 7.____
   A. declaration B. record
   C. payment D. collection
   E. statement

8. Assets are classified as intangible under which of the following conditions? 8.____
   A. They are converted into cash within one year
   B. They have no physical substance
   C. They are acquired in a merger
   D. They are long term and used in operations
   E. They are short term and used in operations

9. Return on assets helps users of financial statements evaluate which of the following? 9.____
   A. Profitability B. Liquidity
   C. Solvency D. Cash flow
   E. Reliability

10. The accounting concept that emphasizes the existence of a business firm separate and apart from its owners is ordinarily termed the ____ concept. 10.____
    A. business separation B. consistency
    C. going-concern D. business materiality
    E. business entity

11. Equity investors are most interested in which aspect(s) of a company? 11.____
    I. Book value
    II. Profitability
    III. Cash flow

    A. I only B. II only
    C. III only D. I and II only
    E. II and III only

12. One disadvantage of the corporation as compared to other types of business organizations is that 12.____
    A. greater legal liability is assigned to stockholders
    B. greater ethical responsibility is expected of officers and employees
    C. greater profit is required by owners
    D. shares of stock can be sold and transferred to new owners
    E. greater tax burden is levied on the entity

13. Land held for future use and not intended for operations should be classified as 13.______
    A. property, plant and equipment
    B. an intangible asset
    C. inventory
    D. an investment
    E. a current asset

14. If an individual borrows $95,000 on July 1 from Community Bank by signing a $95,000, 9 percent, one-year note, what is the accrued interest as of December 31? 14.______
    A. $0
    B. $2,138
    C. $4,275
    D. $6,413
    E. $8,550

15. In the preparation of the Statement of Cash Flows, which of the following transactions will NOT be reported as a financing activity? 15.______
    A. Sale of common stock
    B. Sale of bonds
    C. Issuance of long-term note to bank
    D. Issuance of 30-day note to trade creditor
    E. Purchase of treasury stock

16. A company bought a patent at a cost of $180,000. The patent had an original legal life of 17 years. The remaining legal life is 10 years, but the company expects its useful life will only be six years. When should the cost of the patent be charged to expenses? 16.______
    A. Immediately
    B. Over the next six years
    C. Over the next 10 years
    D. Over the next 17 years
    E. Over the next 40 years

17. How is treasury stock reported on the balance sheet? 17.______
    A. As an increase in liabilities
    B. As an increase in assets
    C. As a decrease in assets
    D. As an increase in stockholders' equity
    E. As a decrease in stockholders' equity

18. The selected accounts below are from TJ Supply's balance sheet. What is TJ Supply's working capital? 18.______

Cash:	$40,000
Accounts receivable:	$120,000
Inventory:	$300,000
Prepaid rent:	$2,000
Accounts payable:	$150,000
Salaries payable:	$7,000
Long-term bonds payable:	$200,000

A. $40,000
B. $105,000
C. $160,000
D. $305,000
E. $462,000

19. A machine with a useful life of eight years was purchased for $600,000 on January 1. The estimated salvage value is $50,000. What is the first year's depreciation by using the double-declining-balance method? 19.______

A. $50,000
B. $68,000
C. $75,000
D. $137,500
E. $150,000

20. Newman Corporation uses the allowance method of accounting for its accounts receivable. The company currently has a $100,000 balance in accounts receivable and a $5,000 balance in its allowance for uncollectible accounts. The company decides to write off $4,000 of its accounts receivable. What would be the balance in its net accounts receivable before and after the write-off? 20.______

	Before	After
A.	$95,000	$91,000
B.	$95,000	$95,000
C.	$100,000	$96,000
D.	$105,000	$101,000
E.	$105,000	$105,000

21. Trading securities must be reported on the balance sheet at 21.______

A. historical cost
B. cost plus earnings minus dividends
C. book value
D. fair market value
E. net present value

22. An accrued expense results in 22.______
    A. an accrued liability
    B. an accrued revenue
    C. a prepaid expense
    D. an unearned revenue
    E. a contra owner's equity account

23. The L Company purchased new machinery and incurred the following costs: 23.______

Invoice price	$30,000
Freight (F.O.B. shipping point)	$2,000
Foundation for machinery	$1,000
Installation costs	$900
Annual maintenance of machinery	$600

The total cost of the machinery is
    A. $30,000
    B. $31,900
    C. $32,000
    D. $33,900
    E. $34,500

24. Which of the following is true of annual depreciation expense? 24.______
    A. It represents the amount required for annual maintenance of a long-term asset
    B. It represents the annual revenue earned by an asset
    C. It allocates the cost of use of a long-term asset to the revenue that it generates
    D. It is required to fulfill the economic entity assumption
    E. It reduces cash

25. The matching concept matches 25.______
    A. customers with businesses
    B. expenses with revenues
    C. assets with liabilities
    D. creditors with businesses
    E. debits with credits

KEY (CORRECT ANSWERS)

1. E	11. E	21. D
2. A	12. E	22. A
3. C	13. D	23. D
4. E	14. C	24. C
5. A	15. D	25. B
6. C	16. B	
7. A	17. E	
8. B	18. D	
9. A	19. E	
10. E	20. B	

EXAMINATION SECTION
TEST 1

DIRECTIONS: Each question or incomplete statement is followed by several suggested answers or completions. Select the one that BEST answers the question or completes the statement. *PRINT THE LETTER OF THE CORRECT ANSWER IN THE SPACE AT THE RIGHT.*

1. Business have computerized accounting systems to 1.____

   A. make better decisions
   B. provide more timely data
   C. provide more accurate data
   D. provide data at lower cost
   E. all of the above

2. Businesses have computerized accounting systems to 2.____

   A. increase managerial effectiveness
   B. reduce operating costs
   C. add confidence and reliability to data
   D. improve effectiveness of clerical worker
   E. all of the above

3. Which accounting system constitutes the entire collection of an organization's accounts? 3.____

   A. AR B. GL C. AP
   D. Payroll E. Order entry

4. Which accounting system tracks money customers or clients owe an organization? 4.____

   A. AR B. GL C. AP
   D. Payroll E. Order entry

5. Which accounting system records money the organization owes others? 5.____

   A. AR B. GL C. AP
   D. Payroll E. Order entry

6. Which accounting system converts hours worked into earnings and determines taxes? 6.____

   A. AR B. GL C. AP
   D. Payroll E. Order entry

7. Which accounting system provides warehouse personnel with picking labels and packing slips? 7.____

   A. AR B. GL C. AP
   D. Payroll E. Order entry

8. Which accounting system tracks a firm's long-term purchases of land, equipment, or buildings? 8.____

   A. Fixed assets B. Order entry
   C. Electronic spreadsheet D. Inventory
   E. Payroll

9. Which accounting system uses a grid of rows and columns to maintain data? 9.____

A. Fixed assets
B. Order entry
C. Electronic spreadsheet
D. Inventory
E. Payroll

10. Which accounting system maintains data about description, cost, vendor, reorder point, and quantities on hand? 10.____

A. Fixed assets
B. Order entry
C. Electronic spreadsheet
D. Inventory
E. Payroll

11. Which accounting system produces the balance sheet? 11.____

A. AR
B. GL
C. AP
D. Payroll
E. Fixed assets

12. Which accounting system produces a statement set to customers or clients listing purchases they have made? 12.____

A. AR
B. GL
C. AP
D. Payroll
E. Fixed assets

13. Which accounting system produces a check sent to vendors to pay for purchases? 13.____

A. AR
B. GL
C. AP
D. Payroll
E. Fixed assets

14. Which accounting system produces the paycheck? 14.____

A. AR
B. GL
C. AP
D. Payroll
E. Fixed assets

15. The transferring of transactions between journals is called 15.____

A. posting
B. credit
C. debit
D. general journal
E. the accounting equation

16. Which represents an increase in an expense account? 16.____

A. Posting
B. Credit
C. Debit
D. General journal
E. The accounting equation

17. Which represents a decrease in an asset or expense account? 17.____

A. Posting
B. Credit
C. Debit
D. General journal
E. The accounting equation

18. Which represents a decrease in a liability account? 18.____

A. Posting
B. Credit
C. Debit
D. General journal
E. The accounting equation

19. Which represents an increase in an asset or liability account? 19.____

A. Posting
B. Credit
C. Debit
D. General journal
E. The accounting equation

20. The chronological list of financial transactions is the 20.____

A. posting
B. credit
C. debit
D. general journal
E. the accounting equation

KEY (CORRECT ANSWERS)

1.	E	11.	B
2.	E	12.	A
3.	B	13.	C
4.	A	14.	D
5.	C	15.	A
6.	D	16.	C
7.	E	17.	B
8.	A	18.	C
9.	C	19.	B
10.	D	20.	D

TEST 2

DIRECTIONS: Each question or incomplete statement is followed by several suggested answers or completions. Select the one that BEST answers the question or completes the statement. *PRINT THE LETTER OF THE CORRECT ANSWER IN THE SPACE AT THE RIGHT.*

1. The double entry accounting system is based on which relationship? 1.____

   A. Posting
   B. Credit
   C. Debit
   D. General journal
   E. The accounting equation

2. Which accounts receivable balancing method tracks only the amount owed? 2.____

   A. Balance forward
   B. Balance only
   C. Closed item
   D. Open item
   E. None of the above

3. Which accounts receivable balancing method posts payments to the oldest transaction first, progressing to the newest transaction? 3.____

   A. Balance forward
   B. Balance only
   C. Closed item
   D. Open item
   E. None of the above

4. Which accounts receivable balancing method permits the customer to specify how the payment will be applied? 4.____

   A. Balance forward
   B. Balance only
   C. Closed item
   D. Open item
   E. None of the above

5. One of the advantages of tracking the age of a customer's debt is to 5.____

   A. promote prompt payment
   B. determine the customer's reliability
   C. assist in debt collection
   D. advise management of likelihood of debt collection
   E. all of the above

6. Which of the following is input to an accounts payable system? 6.____

   A. Customer statements
   B. General journal
   C. Vendor's check
   D. Voucher
   E. None of the above

7. Which of the following is input to an accounts payable system? 7.____

   A. Customer statements
   B. General journal
   C. Vendor check
   D. Invoice
   E. None of the above

8. What is the PRIMARY input to a payroll system? 8.____

   A. Voucher
   B. Time card
   C. Invoice
   D. Vendor check
   E. Customer statement

9. What is the PRIMARY input to an accounts receivable system? 9.____

A. Voucher
B. Credit sales receipt
C. Invoice
D. Vendor check
E. Customer statement

10. Which of the following terms do NOT apply to an electronic spreadsheet? 10.____

A. Row
B. Cell
C. Column
D. Debit
E. Formula

11. Which of the following terms do NOT apply to an electronic spreadsheet? 11.____

A. Row
B. Cell
C. Text
D. Sum
E. Average

12. The third column and the fourth row of a spreadsheet is named ______. 12.____

A. D3
B. D4
C. 4D
D. 3D
E. None of the above

13. Electronic spreadsheets label rows with ______. 13.____

A. letters
B. names
C. rows
D. numbers
E. columns

14. Order entry is USUALLY a part of ______. 14.____

A. AP
B. GL
C. AR
D. Payroll
E. None of the above

15. Fixed asset systems assist a business by 15.____

A. tracking repair histories
B. providing tax depreciation data
C. determining optimal replacement times
D. assisting with insurance needs
E. all of the above

16. An order entry system is CLOSELY related to a(n) ______ system. 16.____

A. inventory
B. AP
C. payroll
D. fixed asset
E. all of the above

17. The intersection of a row and column in an electronic spreadsheet is called a(n) 17.____

A. union
B. debit
C. cell
D. function
E. RC

18. Which system provides management with information on potential discounts that may be available to them? 18.____

A. AR
B. AP
C. Payroll
D. GL
E. Order entry

19. Which system does NOT interact with the GL? 19.____

A. AR
B. AP
C. Payroll
D. Fixed assets
E. None of the above

20. Which accounting system generates the profit and loss statement? 20.____

A. AP B. AR C. Payroll
D. GL E. Balance sheet

KEY (CORRECT ANSWERS)

1.	E	11.	C
2.	B	12.	B
3.	A	13.	D
4.	D	14.	C
5.	E	15.	E
6.	D	16.	A
7.	D	17.	C
8.	B	18.	B
9.	B	19.	E
10.	D	20.	D

EXAMINATION SECTION

TEST 1

DIRECTIONS: Each question or incomplete statement is followed by several suggested answers or completions. Select the one that BEST answers the question or completes the statement. *PRINT THE LETTER OF THE CORRECT ANSWER IN THE SPACE AT THE RIGHT.*

1. Which one of the following is considered a word processor program? 1.____
   A. Microsoft Word B. Microsoft Works
   C. Notepad D. Both A and B

2. Default headings are available under the _____ tab. 2.____
   A. Insert B. Home C. File D. View

3. _____ deals with font, alignment and margins. 3.____
   A. Selecting B. Formatting C. Composing D. Pattern

4. Which one of the following is the BEST format for storing bit-mapped images on the computer? 4.____
   A. .JPG B. .PNG C. .GIF D. .TIF

5. A header specifies an area in the _____ margins of every page. 5.____
   A. top B. bottom C. left D. right

6. When an Excel file is inserted into a Word document, the data is 6.____
   A. hyperlinked B. placed in a Word table
   C. linked D. embedded

7. A workbook in Excel is a file that 7.____
   A. is primarily used to generate graphs
   B. is often used for word processing
   C. can contain many sheets, chart sheets and worksheets
   D. both A and B

8. Excel can produce chart types that include 8.____
   A. only line graphs
   B. bar charts, line graphs and pie charts
   C. line graphs and pie charts only
   D. bar charts and line graphs only

9. In PowerPoint, the motion path is a 9.____
   A. method of moving items on the slide
   B. method of advancing slides
   C. indentation
   D. type of animation

10. _____ replaces similar words in a document. 10.____
    A. Word Count B. Thesaurus C. Wrap Text D. Format Printer

11. The MOST simple description of the Internet is 11.____
    A. a single network
    B. a huge collection of different networks
    C. collection of LANs
    D. single WAN

12. How can a computer be connected to the Internet? 12.____
    A. Through internet service providers B. Internet society
    C. Internet architecture board D. Local area network

13. A software program that is used to view web pages is known as a(n) 13.____
    A. Internet browser B. interpreter
    C. operating system D. website

14. Which of the following is used to search anything on the Internet? 14.____
    A. Search engines B. Routers
    C. Social networks D. Websites

15. When a website is accessed, its main page is called 15.____
    A. home page B. back end page
    C. dead end D. both A and B

16. Google Docs provides _____, which is a salient feature of Google Doc. 16.____
    A. image processing B. synchronization
    C. both A and B D. installation

17. Documents in Google Drive could be accessed from 17.____
    A. only a personal computer
    B. any computer that has Internet connection
    C. only that computer that has Google drive on hard disk
    D. both B and C

18. In an email address, for example test@gmail.com, "gmail" is known as 18.____
    A. domain
    B. host computer in commercial domain
    C. internet service provider
    D. URL

19. Which of the following is NOT a well-known domain? 19.____
    A. .edu B. .com C. .org D. .army

20. Cyberspace is an alternative name used for 20.____
    A. Internet B. information C. virtual space D. data space

21. Which one of the following is NOT an Internet browser? 21.____
    A. Chrome B. Firefly C. Firefox D. Safari

22. Which of the following is NOT a past or current search engine? 22.____
    A. Apple B. Lycos C. Bing D. Google

23. Document scanning could be done through 23.____
    A. OCR B. OMR
    C. both A and B D. dot-matrix printer

24. _____ are used to fill out empty fields in scanned images of data. 24.____
    A. Computerized optical scanners B. OCR software
    C. Scanners D. Laser printers

25. All of the following are examples of hardware for standard home use EXCEPT 25.____
    A. flash drives B. inkjet printers
    C. servers D. laser printers

KEY (CORRECT ANSWERS)

1.	D	11.	B
2.	B	12.	A
3.	B	13.	A
4.	D	14.	A
5.	A	15.	A
6.	B	16.	B
7.	C	17.	B
8.	B	18.	B
9.	A	19.	D
10.	B	20.	A

21.	B
22.	A
23.	C
24.	A
25.	C

TEST 2

DIRECTIONS: Each question or incomplete statement is followed by several suggested answers or completions. Select the one that BEST answers the question or completes the statement. *PRINT THE LETTER OF THE CORRECT ANSWER IN THE SPACE AT THE RIGHT.*

1. In a spreadsheet, data is organized in the form of 1.____
   A. lines and spaces
   B. rows and columns
   C. layers and planes
   D. height and width

2. Which one of the following menus is used to protect a worksheet? 2.____
   A. Edit
   B. Format
   C. Data
   D. Tools

3. _____ corrects spelling mistakes automatically. 3.____
   A. Word wrap
   B. AutoCorrect
   C. Spell checker
   D. Thesaurus

4. Which function is used to automatically align text? 4.____
   A. Justification
   B. Indentation
   C. Both A and B
   D. None of the above

5. Orientation is the property of the _____ function. 5.____
   A. Print
   B. Design
   C. Image
   D. Both A and B

6. Special effects that are used to present slides in a presentation are known as 6.____
   A. effects
   B. custom animation
   C. transition
   D. present animation

7. Page setup and print functions can typically be found in the ____ menu. 7.____
   A. tools
   B. format
   C. file
   D. edit

8. Which one of the following is considered removable storage media? 8.____
   A. Scanner
   B. Flash drive
   C. External hard drive
   D. Both B and C

9. Which component of the computer is called the brain of the computer? 9.____
   A. ALU
   B. Memory
   C. Control Unit
   D. CPU

10. .txt is a file that is named for _____ files. 10.____
    A. Notepad
    B. Word
    C. Paint
    D. Excel

11. Software programs that are automatically downloaded and work within a browser are known as 11.____
    A. plug-in
    B. utilities
    C. widgets
    D. add-on

12. _____ is a computer that requests data from other computers on the Internet. 12.____
    A. Client   B. Server
    C. Super computer   D. Personal computer

13. A wizard is considered as a _____ file with prompt display. 13.____
    A. system   B. program   C. help   D. application

14. E-mails from unknown senders go into the _____ folder. 14.____
    A. Spam   B. Trash   C. Drafts   D. Inbox

15. LAN is an abbreviation for _____ area network. 15.____
    A. line   B. local   C. large   D. limited

16. Which of the following is NOT an extension for an image file? 16.____
    A. .bmp   B. .jpg   C. .png   D. .xls

17. In the e-mail address *test@gmail.com*, "test" is the _____ name. 17.____
    A. domain   B. user   C. server   D. ISP

18. To e-mail multiple recipients while hiding the recipients from view, use the ___ function. 18.____
    A. BCC   B. CC   C. send   D. hide

19. The system that translates an IP address into a simple form that is easy to remember is 19.____
    A. domain name system   B. domain
    C. domain numbering system   D. server domain

20. Which one of the following is the CORRECT method to send a file through e-mail? 20.____
    A. CC   B. Attachment
    C. Embed through HTML   D. Both A and B

21. Inkjet printers are categorized as a(n) _____ printer. 21.____
    A. character   B. ink   C. line   D. band

22. Which one of the following is a storage medium that has a shape of a circular plate? 22.____
    A. Disk   B. CPU   C. ALU   D. Printer

23. Ctrl+P activates the ______ function. 23.____
    A. reboot   B. save   C. print   D. paint

24. The file extension .exe represents an _____ file. 24.____
    A. examination   B. extra   C. executable   D. extension

25. Which of the following is NOT considered an input device? 25.____
A. OCR
B. Optical scanner
C. Printer
D. Keyboard

KEY (CORRECT ANSWERS)

1. B
2. D
3. B
4. A
5. A

6. C
7. C
8. D
9. D
10. A

11. B
12. A
13. C
14. A
15. B

16. D
17. B
18. A
19. A
20. B

21. C
22. A
23. C
24. C
25. C

TEST 3

DIRECTIONS: Each question or incomplete statement is followed by several suggested answers or completions. Select the one that BEST answers the question or completes the statement. *PRINT THE LETTER OF THE CORRECT ANSWER IN THE SPACE AT THE RIGHT.*

1. Excel is a _____ program. 1.____
   A. graphics B. word processor
   C. spreadsheet D. typewriter

2. Basically, a word processor program like Microsoft Word is a replacement for 2.____
   A. manual work B. typewriters
   C. both A and B D. graphical programs

3. Which one of the following could be added as a sound effect to a PowerPoint presentation? 3.____
   A. .wav files and.mid files B. .wav files and .gif files
   C. .wav files and .jpg files D. .jpg files and .gif files

4. Google Drive is an example of _____ software. 4.____
   A. system B. application C. database D. firmware

5. PDF stands for _____ document format. 5.____
   A. portable B. picture C. plain D. private

6. Which one of the following is an example of internal memory of a computer? 6.____
   A. Disks B. Pen drive C. RAM D. CDs

7. A keyboard is an example of a(n) _____ device. 7.____
   A. input B. output
   C. word processor D. printing

8. Clip art is a collection of _____ that can be inserted into a document. 8.____
   A. text files B. image files
   C. templates D. audio files

9. _____ is a distinctive part of memory which holds the contents temporarily during cut or copy functions. 9.____
   A. Clipboard B. Macro C. Template D. Clip art

10. _____ is a process to store files on a computer from the Internet. 10.____
    A. Uploading B. Downloading
    C. Pulling D. Transferring

11. "Cut and paste" refers to 11.____
    A. deleting and moving text B. restoring and updating software
    C. cleaning images D. replacing images

12. Which one of the following is a compressed format for images? 12.____
A. GIF B. JPGE C. PNG D. JPG

13. A computer stores information and data inside the 13.____
A. hard drive B. CPU C. CD D. monitor

14. WWW is an abbreviation of 14.____
A. world wide web B. wide world web
C. web worldwide D. world wide website

15. A _____ computer holds more than one processor. 15.____
A. multithread B. multi-unit
C. multiprocessor D. multiprogramming

16. Landscape and portrait are properties of 16.____
A. page layout B. design C. formatting D. text

17. _____ includes the company's name, address, phone number and e-mail address. 17.____
A. Letterhead B. Template C. Visiting Card D. Brochure

18. _____ Server provides database services for other computers. 18.____
A. Application B. Web C. Database D. FTP

19. Which one of the following is responsible for storing movies, images and pictures? 19.____
A. File server B. Web server
C. Database server D. Application server

20. GUI stands for graphical 20.____
A. user interface B. unified instrument
C. unified interface D. user instrument

21. Scanner is an example of a(n) _____ device. 21.____
A. output B. input C. printing D. both A and B

22. Which one of the following is NOT an example of computer hardware? 22.____
A. Printer B. Scanner C. Mouse D. Antivirus

23. Which one of the following provides the BEST quality reproduction of graphics? 23.____
A. Laser printer B. Inkjet printer
C. Dot-matrix printer D. Plotter

24. If an e-mail sender is unknown, then do not download the _____ because it might contain a virus. 24.____
A. attachment B. email
C. spam D. both A and B

25. The BEST way to send identical emails to more than one person is to 25.____
    A. use the CC option B. add email ID to address
    C. forward D. both A and B

KEY (CORRECT ANSWERS)

1.	C	11.	A
2.	B	12.	A
3.	A	13.	A
4.	B	14.	A
5.	A	15.	C
6.	C	16.	A
7.	A	17.	A
8.	B	18.	C
9.	A	19.	A
10.	B	20.	A

21.	B
22.	D
23.	D
24.	A
25.	A

TEST 4

DIRECTIONS: Each question or incomplete statement is followed by several suggested answers or completions. Select the one that BEST answers the question or completes the statement. *PRINT THE LETTER OF THE CORRECT ANSWER IN THE SPACE AT THE RIGHT.*

1. A keyboard shortcut for saving files is 1.____
   A. Alt+S B. Ctrl+S C. Ctrl+SV D. S+Enter

2. Which of the following is NOT a term relevant to Excel? 2.____
   A. slide B. cell
   C. formula D. column

3. A _____ background is a grainy and non-smooth surface. 3.____
   A. texture B. gradient C. solid D. pattern

4. Word wrap forces all text to fit within the defined 4.____
   A. margin B. indent C. block D. box

5. In Microsoft Word, overview of the prepared document could be better seen through 5.____
   A. Preview B. Print Preview
   C. Review D. both A and B

6. The amount of vertical space between text line in a document is known as 6.____
   A. double space B. line spacing
   C. single space D. vertical spacing

7. Which one of the following devices is required for Internet connection? 7.____
   A. Joy stick B. Modem C. NIC card D. Optical drive

8. IBM is a short form used for 8.____
   A. Internal Business Management
   B. International Business Management
   C. Internal Business Machines
   D. International Business Machines

9. Which one of the following is static and non-volatile memory? 9.____
   A. RAM B. ROM C. BIOS D. Cache

10. One disadvantage of Google Docs is 10.____
    A. less storage B. compatibility
    C. needs connectivity to Internet D. synchronization

11. WAN is an abbreviation of _____ area network. 11.____
    A. wide B. wired C. whole D. while

12. Bibliography can be created through the _____ tab. 12.____
    A. References B. Design C. Review D. Insert

13. The _____ is MOST likely shared in a computer network. 13.____
    A. keyboard B. speaker C. printer D. scanner

14. A normal computer is not able to boot if it does not have a(n) 14.____
    A. operating system B. complier
    C. loader D. assembler

15. _____ is another name for junk e-mails. 15.____
    A. Spam B. Spoof C. Spool D. Sniffer scripts

16. A table of contents can be created automatically by using an option in 16.____
    A. Page Layout B. Insert C. References D. View

17. ALU stands for 17.____
    A. arithmetic logic unit B. array logic unit
    C. application logic unit D. both A and B

18. Orientation is concerned with the _____ set-up of the page. 18.____
    A. horizontal B. vertical C. both A and B D. spacing

19. _____ is a form of written communication within the same company which comprises guide words as heading. 19.____
    A. Memorandum B. Letterhead
    C. Template D. None of the above

20. Which one of the following is NOT a web browser? 20.____
    A. Chrome B. Opera C. Firefox D. Drupal

21. .net domain is specifically used for 21.____
    A. international organization
    B. internet infrastructure and service providers
    C. educational institutes
    D. commercial business

22. A modem is not required when the Internet is connected through 22.____
    A. Wi-Fi B. LAN
    C. dial-up phone D. cable

23. Mail Merge uses _____ to create separate copies of a document for multiple people in Microsoft Word. 23.____
    A. primary document B. data document
    C. both A and B D. web page

24. Linux is an example of 24.____
    A. operating system B. malware
    C. firmware D. application program

25. Which one of the following is a CORRECT format for a website address? 25.____
    A. www@com
    B. www.test.com
    C. www.test25A@com
    D. www#TeST.com

KEY (CORRECT ANSWERS)

1.	B	11.	A
2.	A	12.	A
3.	B	13.	C
4.	A	14.	A
5.	B	15.	A
6.	B	16.	C
7.	B	17.	A
8.	D	18.	C
9.	B	19.	A
10.	C	20.	D

21.	B
22.	A
23.	C
24.	A
25.	B

READING COMPREHENSION
UNDERSTANDING WRITTEN MATERIALS

COMMENTARY

The ability to read and understand written materials—texts, publications, newspapers, orders, directions, expositions—is a skill basic to a functioning democracy and to an efficient business or viable government.

That is why almost all examinations—for beginning, middle, and senior levels—test reading comprehension, directly or indirectly.

The reading test measures how well you understand what you read. This is how it is done: You read a passage followed by several statements. From these statements, you choose the one statement, or answer, that is BEST supported by, or BEST matches, what is said in the paragraph. PRINT THE LETTER OF THE CORRECT ANSWER IN THE SPACE AT THE RIGHT.

SAMPLE QUESTION

DIRECTIONS: Answer Question 1 ONLY according to the information given in the following passage.

1. A cashier has to make many arithmetic calculations in connection with his work. Skill in arithmetic comes readily with practice; no special talent is needed. 1.____
On the basis of the above statement, it is MOST accurate to state that
   A. the most important part of a cashier's job is to make calculations
   B. few cashiers have the special ability needed to handle arithmetic problems easily
   C. without special talent, cashiers cannot learn to do the calculations they are required to do in their work
   D. a cashier can, with practice, learn to handle the computations he is required to make

The CORRECT answer is D.

EXAMINATION SECTION

TEST 1

DIRECTIONS: Questions 1 through 5 are to be answered on the basis of the following reading passage. *PRINT THE LETTER OF THE CORRECT ANSWER IN THE SPACE AT THE RIGHT.*

The size of each collection route will be determined by the amount of waste per stop, distance between stops, speed of loading, speed of truck, traffic conditions during loading time, etc.

Basically, the route should consist of a proper amount of work for a crew for the daily work period. The crew should service all properties eligible for this service in their area. Routes should, whenever practical, be compact, with a logical progression through the area. Unnecessary travel should be avoided. Traffic conditions on the route should be thoroughly studied to prevent lost time in loading, to reduce hazards to employees, and to minimize tying up of regular traffic movements by collection forces. Natural and physical barriers and arterial streets should be used as route boundaries wherever possible to avoid lost time in travel.

Routes within a district should be laid out so that the crews start at the point farthest from the disposal area and, as the day progresses, move toward that area, thus reducing the length of the haul. When possible, the work of the crews in a district should be parallel as they progress throughout the day, with routes finishing up within a short distance of each other. This enables the supervisor to be present when crews are completing their work and enables him to shift crews to trouble spots to complete the day's work.

1. Based on the above passage, an advantage of having collection routes end near one another is that 1.____
   A. routes can be made more compact
   B. unnecessary travel is avoided, saving manpower
   C. the length of the haul is reduced
   D. the supervisor can exercise better manpower control

2. Of the factors mentioned above which affect the size of a collection route, the two over which the sanitation forces have LEAST control are 2.____
   A. amount of waste; traffic conditions
   B. speed of loading; amount of waste
   C. speed of truck; distance between stops
   D. traffic conditions; speed of truck

3. According to the above passage, the size of a collection route is probably good if 3.____
   A. it is a fair day's work for a normal crew
   B. it is not necessary for the trucks to travel too fast
   C. the amount of waste collected can be handled properly
   D. the distance between stops is approximately equal

4. Based on the above passage, it is reasonable to assume that a sanitation officer laying out collection routes should NOT try to have 4.____
   A. an arterial street as a route boundary
   B. any routes near the disposal area
   C. the routes overlap a little
   D. the routes run in the same direction

5. The term "logical progression," as used in the second paragraph of the passage refers MOST NEARLY to 5.____
   A. collecting from street after street in order
   B. numbering streets one after the other
   C. rotating crew assignments
   D. using logic as a basis for assigned crews

KEY (CORRECT ANSWERS)

1. D
2. A
3. A
4. C
5. A

TEST 2

DIRECTIONS: Questions 1 through 3 are to be answered on the basis of the following reading passage. *PRINT THE LETTER OF THE CORRECT ANSWER IN THE SPACE AT THE RIGHT.*

In an open discussion designed to arrive at solutions to community problems, the person leading the discussion group should give the members a chance to make their suggestions before he makes his. He must not be afraid of silence; if he talks just to keep things going, he will find he can't stop, and good discussion will not develop. In other words, the more he talks, the more the group will depend on him. If he finds, however, that no one seems ready to begin the discussion, his best "opening" is to ask for definitions of terms which form the basis of the discussion. By pulling out as many definitions or interpretations as possible, he can get the group started "thinking out load," which is essential to good discussion.

1. According to the above passage, good group discussion is MOST likely to result if the person leading the discussion group 1.____
   A. keeps the discussion going by speaking whenever the group stops speaking
   B. encourages the group to depend on him by speaking more than any other group member
   C. makes his own suggestions before the group has a chance to make theirs
   D. encourages discussion by asking the group to interpret the terms to be discussed

2. According to the above passage, "thinking out loud" by the discussion group is 2.____
   A. *good* practice, because "thinking out loud" is important to good discussion
   B. *poor* practice, because group members should think out their ideas before discussing them
   C. *good* practice, because it will encourage the person leading the discussion to speak more
   D. *poor* practice, because it causes the group to fear silence during discussion

3. According to the above passage, the one of the following which is LEAST desirable at an open discussion is having 3.____
   A. silent periods during which none of the group members speaks
   B. differences of opinion among the group members concerning the definition of terms
   C. a discussion leader who uses "openings" to get the discussion started
   D. a discussion leader who provides all suggestions and definitions for the group

KEY (CORRECT ANSWERS)

1. D
2. A
3. D

TEST 3

DIRECTIONS: Questions 1 through 4 are to be answered on the basis of the following reading passage. *PRINT THE LETTER OF THE CORRECT ANSWER IN THE SPACE AT THE RIGHT.*

The insects you will control are just a minute fraction of the millions which inhabit the world. Man does well to hold his own in the face of the constant pressures that insects continue to exert upon him. Not only are the total numbers tremendous, but the number of individual kinds, or species, certainly exceeds 800,000—number greater than that of all other animals combined. Many of these are beneficial but some are especially competitive with man. Not only are insects numerous, but they are among the most adaptable of all animals. In their many forms, they are fitted for almost any specific way of life. Their adaptability, combined with their tremendous rate of reproduction, gives insects an unequaled potential for survival!

The food of insects includes almost anything that can be eaten by any other animal as well as many things which cannot even be digested by any other animals. Most insects do not harm the products of man or carry diseases harmful to him; however, many do carry diseases and others feed on his food and manufactured goods. Some are adapted to living only in open areas while others are able to live in extremely confined spaces. All of these factor combined make the insects a group of animals having many members which are a nuisance to man and thus of great importance.

The control of insects requires an understanding of their way of life. Thus, it is necessary to understand the anatomy of the insect, its method of growth, the time it takes for the insect to grow from egg to adult, its habits, the stage of its life history in which it causes damage, its food, and its common living places. In order to obtain the best control, it is especially important to be able to identify correctly the specific insect involved because, without this knowledge, it is impossible to prescribe a proper treatment.

1. Which one of the following is a CORRECT statement about the insect population of the world, according to the above passage? The 1.____
   A. total number of insects is less than the total number of all other animals combined
   B. number of species of insects is greater than the number of species of all other animals combined
   C. total number of harmful insects is less than the number of species of those which are harmful
   D. number of species of harmless insects is less than the number of species of those which are harmful

2. Insects will be controlled MOST efficiently if you 2.____
   A. understand why the insects are so numerous
   B. know what insects you are dealing with
   C. see if the insects compete with man
   D. are able to identify the food which the insects digest

3. According to the above passage, insects are of importance to a scientist PRIMARILY because they 3.____
   A. can be annoying, destructive, and harmful to man
   B. are able to thrive in very small spaces
   C. cause damage during their growth stages
   D. are so adaptable that they can adjust to any environment

4. According to the above passage, insects can eat 4.____
   A. everything that any other living thing can eat
   B. man's food and thing which he makes
   C. anything which other animals can't digest
   D. only food and food products

KEY (CORRECT ANSWERS)

1. B
2. B
3. A
4. B

TEST 4

DIRECTIONS: Questions 1 through 3 are to be answered on the basis of the following reading passage. *PRINT THE LETTER OF THE CORRECT ANSWER IN THE SPACE AT THE RIGHT.*

Telephone service in a government agency should be adequate and complete with respect to information given or action taken. It must be remembered that telephone contacts should receive special consideration since the caller cannot see the operator. People like to feel that they are receiving personal attention and that their requests or criticisms are receiving individual rather than routine consideration. All this contributes to what has come to be known as *tone of service*. The aim is to use standards which are clearly very good or superior. The factors to be considered in determining what makes good tone of service are speech, courtesy, understanding, and explanations. A caller's impression of tone of service will affect the general public attitude toward the agency and city services in general.

1. The above passage states that people who telephone a government agency like to feel that they are 1.____
   A. creating a positive image of themselves
   B. being given routine consideration
   C. receiving individual attention
   D. setting standards for telephone service

2. Which one of the following is NOT mentioned in the above passage as a factor in determining good tone of service? 2.____
   A. Courtesy B. Education C. Speech D. Understanding

3. The above passage implies that failure to properly handle telephone calls is MOST likely to result in 3.____
   A. a poor impression of city agencies by the public
   B. a deterioration of courtesy toward operators
   C. an effort by operators to improve the Tone of Service
   D. special consideration by the public of operator difficulties

KEY (CORRECT ANSWERS)

1. C
2. B
3. A

TEST 5

DIRECTIONS: Questions 1 through 5 are to be answered on the basis of the following reading passage. *PRINT THE LETTER OF THE CORRECT ANSWER IN THE SPACE AT THE RIGHT.*

For some office workers it is useful to be familiar with the four main classes of domestic mail; for others, it is essential. Each class has a different rate of postage and some have requirements concerning wrapping, sealing, or special information to be placed on the package.

First-class mail, the class which may not be opened for postal inspection, includes letters, postcards, business reply cards, and other kinds of written matter. There are different rates for some of the kinds of cards which can be sent by first-class mail. The maximum weight for an item sent by first-class mail is 70 pounds. An item which is not letter size should be marked "First Class: on all sides.

Although office workers most often come into contact with first-class mail, they may find it helpful to know something about the other classes. Second-class mail is generally used for mailing newspapers and magazines. Publishers of these articles must meet certain U.S. Postal Service requirements in order to obtain a permit to use second-class mailing rates. Third-class mail, which must weigh less than 1 pound, includes printed materials and merchandise parcels. There are two rate structure for this class, a single-piece rate and a bulk rate. Fourth-class mail, also known as parcel post, includes packages weighing from one to 40 pounds. For more information about these classes of mail and the actual mailing rates, contact our local post office.

1. According to this passage, first-class mail is the only class which 1.____
   A. has a limit on the maximum weight of an item
   B. has different rates for items within the class
   C. may not be opened for postal inspection
   D. should be used by office workers

2. According to this passage, the one of the following items which may CORRECTLY be sent by fourth-class mail is a 2.____
   A. magazine weighing one-half pound
   B. package weighing one-half pound
   C. package weighing two pounds
   D. postcard

3. According to this passage, there are different postage rates for 3.____
   A. a newspaper sent by second-class mail and a magazine sent by second-class mail
   B. each of the classes of mail
   C. each pound of fourth-class mail
   D. printed material sent by third-class mail and merchandise parcels sent by third-class mail

4. In order to send a newspaper by second-class mail, a publisher must 4.____
   A. have met certain postal requirements and obtained a permit
   B. indicate whether he wants to use the single-piece or the bulk rate
   C. make certain that the newspaper weighs less than one pound
   D. mark the newspaper "Second Class" on the top and bottom of the wrapper

5. Of the following types of information, the one which is NOT mentioned in the passage is the 5.____
   A. class of mail to which parcel post belongs
   B. kinds of items which can be sent by each class of mail
   C. maximum weight for an item sent by fourth-class mail
   D. postage rate for each of the four classes of mail

KEY (CORRECT ANSWERS)

1. C
2. C
3. B
4. A
5. D

TEST 6

DIRECTIONS: Questions 1 through 5 are to be answered on the basis of the following reading passage. *PRINT THE LETTER OF THE CORRECT ANSWER IN THE SPACE AT THE RIGHT.*

The thickness of insulation necessary for the most economical results varies with the steam temperature. The standard covering consists of 85 percent magnesia with 10 percent of long-fibre asbestos as a binder. Both magnesia and laminated asbestos-felt and other forms of mineral wool including glass wool are also used for heat insulation. The magnesia and laminated-asbestos coverings may be safely used at temperatures up to 600ºF. Pipe insulation is applied in molded sections 3 feet long; the sections are attached to the pipe by means of galvanized iron wire or netting. Flanges and fittings can be insulated by direct application of magnesia cement to the metal without *reinforcement*. Insulation should always be maintained inn good condition because it saves fuel. Routine maintenance of warm-pipe insulation should include prompt repair of damaged surfaces. Steam and hot-water leaks concealed by insulation will be difficult to detect. Underground steam or hot-water pipes are best insulated using a concrete trench with removable cover.

1. The word *reinforcement*, as used above, means MOST NEARLY 1.____
   A. resistance B. strengthening
   C. regulation D. removal

2. According to the above paragraph, magnesia and laminated asbestos coverings may be safely used at temperatures up to 2.____
   A. 800ºF B. 720ºF C. 675ºF D. 600ºF

3. According to the above paragraph, insulation should *always* be maintained in good condition because it 3.____
   A. is laminated B. saves fuel
   C. is attached to the pipe D. prevents leaks

4. According to the above paragraph, pipe insulation sections are attached to the pipe by means of 4.____
   A. binders B. mineral wool
   C. netting D. staples

5. According to the above paragraph, a leak in a hot-water pipe may be difficult to detect because, when insulation is used, the leak is 5.____
   A. underground B. hidden C. routine D. cemented

KEY (CORRECT ANSWERS)

1. B
2. D
3. B
4. C
5. B

TEST 7

DIRECTIONS: Questions 1 through 4 are to be answered on the basis of the following reading passage. *PRINT THE LETTER OF THE CORRECT ANSWER IN THE SPACE AT THE RIGHT.*

Cylindrical surfaces are the most common form of finished surfaces found on machine parts, although flat surfaces are also very common; hence, many metal-cutting processes are for the purpose of producing either cylindrical or flat surfaces. The machines used for cylindrical or flat shapes may be, and often are, utilized also for forming the various irregular or special shapes required on many machine parts. Because of the prevalence of cylindrical and flat surfaces, the student of manufacturing practice should learn first about the machines and methods employed to produce these surfaces. The cylindrical surfaces may be internal as in holes and cylinders. Any one part may, of course, have cylindrical sections of different diameters and lengths and include flat ends or shoulders and, frequently, there is a threaded part or, possibly, some finished surface that is not circular in cross-section. The prevalence of cylindrical surfaces on machine parts explains why lathes are found in all machine shops. It is important to understand the various uses of the lathes because many of the operations are the same fundamentally as those performed on other types of machine tools.

1. According to the above passage, the MOST common form of finished surfaces found on machine parts is 1.____
   A. cylindrical B. elliptical C. flat D. square

2. According to the above passage, any one part of cylindrical surfaces may have 2.____
   A. chases B. shoulders C. keyways D. splines

3. According to the above passage, lathes are found in all machine shops because cylindrical surfaces on machine parts are 3.____
   A. scarce B. internal C. common D. external

4. As used in the above paragraph, the word *processes* means 4.____
   A. operations B. purposes C. devices D. tools

KEY (CORRECT ANSWERS)

1. A
2. B
3. C
4. A

TEST 8

DIRECTIONS: Questions 1 and 2 are to be answered on the basis of the following reading passage. *PRINT THE LETTER OF THE CORRECT ANSWER IN THE SPACE AT THE RIGHT.*

The principle of interchangeability requires manufacture to such specification that component parts of a device may be selected at random and assembled to fit and operate satisfactorily. Interchangeable manufacture, therefore, requires that parts be made to definite limits of error, and to fit gages instead of mating parts. Interchangeability does not necessarily involve a high degree of precision; stove lids, for example, are interchangeable but are not particularly accurate, and carriage bolts and nuts are not precision products but are completely interchangeable. Interchangeability may be employed in unit-production as well as mass-production systems of manufacture.

1. According to the above paragraph, in order for parts to be interchangeable, they must be 1.____
   A. precision-machined B. selectively-assembled
   C. mass-produced D. made to fit gages

2. According to the above paragraph, carriage bolts are interchangeable because they are 2.____
   A. precision-made B. sized to specific tolerances
   C. individually matched products D. produced in small units

---

KEY (CORRECT ANSWERS)

1. D
2. B

ARITHMETICAL REASONING

EXAMINATION SECTION

TEST 1

DIRECTIONS: Each question or incomplete statement is followed by several suggested answers or completions. Select the one that BEST answers the question or completes the statement. *PRINT THE LETTER OF THE CORRECT ANSWER IN THE SPACE AT THE RIGHT.*

1. The ABC Corporation had a gross income of $125,500.00 in 2019. Of this, it paid 60% for overhead. 1.____
If the gross income for 2020 increased by $6,500 and the cost of overhead increased to 61% of gross income, how much MORE did it pay for overhead in 2020 than in 2019?
A. $1,320 B. $5,220 C. $7,530 D. $8,052

2. After one year, Mr. Richards paid back a total of $16,950 as payment for a $15,000 loan. All the money paid over $15,000 was simple interest. 2.____
The interest charge was MOST NEARLY
A. 13% B. 11% C. 9% D. 7%

3. A checking account has a balance of $253.36. 3.____
If deposits of $36.95, $210.23, and $7.34 and withdrawals of $117.35, $23.37, and $15.98 are made, what is the NEW balance of the account?
A. $155.54 B. $351.18 C. $364.58 D. $664.58

4. In 2020, the W Realty Company spent 27% of its income on rent. 4.____
If it earned $97,254 in 2020, the amount it paid for rent was
A. $26,258.58 B. 26,348.58 C. $27,248.58 D. $27,358.58

5. Six percent simple annual interest on $2,436.18 is MOST NEARLY 5.____
A. $145.08 B. $145.17 C. $146.08 D. $146.17

6. H. Partridge receives a weekly gross salary (before deductions) of $397.50. 6.____
Through weekly payroll deductions of $13.18, he is paying back a loan he took from his pension fund.
If other fixed weekly deductions amount to $122.76, how much pay would Mr. Partridge take home over a period of 33 weeks?
A. $7,631.28 B. $8,250.46 C. $8,631.48 D. $13,117.50

7. Mr. Robertson is a city employee enrolled in a city retirement system. He has taken out a loan from the retirement fund and is paying it back at the rate of $14.90 every two weeks. 7.____
In eighteen weeks, how much money will he have paid back on the loan?
A. $268.20 B. $152.80 C. $134.10 D. $67.05

8. In 2019, The Iridor Book Company had the following expenses: rent, \$6,500; overhead, \$52,585; inventory, \$35,700; and miscellaneous, \$1,275. 8.____
If all of these expenses went up 18% in 2020, what would they TOTAL in 2020?
A. \$17,290.80 B. \$78,769.20 C. \$96,060.00 D. \$113,350.80

9. Ms. Ranier had a gross salary of \$710.72 paid once every two weeks. 9.____
If the deductions from each paycheck are \$125.44, \$50.26, \$12.58, and \$2.54, how much money would Ms. Ranier take home in eight weeks?
A. \$2,079.60 B. \$2,842.88 C. \$4,159.20 D. \$5,685.76

10. Mr. Martin had a net income of \$95,500 in 2019. 10.____
If he spent 34% on rent and household expenses, 3% on house furnishings, 25% on clothes, and 36% on food, how much was left for savings and other expenses?
A. \$980 B. \$1,910 C. \$3,247 D. \$9,800

11. Mr. Elsberg can pay back a loan of \$1,800 from the city employees' retirement system if he pays back \$36.69 every two weeks for two full years. 11.____
At the end of the two years, how much more than the original \$1,800 he borrowed will Mr. Elsberg have paid back?
A. \$53.94 B. \$107.88 C. \$190.79 D. \$214.76

12. Mr. Nusbaum is a city employee receiving a gross salary (salary before deductions) of \$20,800. Every two weeks, the following deductions are taken out of his salary: Federal Income Tax, \$162.84; FICA, \$44.26; State Tax, \$29.2; City Tax, \$13.94; Health Insurance, \$3.14. 12.____
If Mr. Nusbaum's salary and deductions remained the same for a full calendar year, what would his net salary (gross salary less deductions) be in that year?
A. \$6,596.20 B. \$14,198.60 C. \$18,745.50 D. \$20,546.30

13. Add: 8936, 7821, 8953, 4297, 9785, 6579. 13.____
A. 45,371 B. 45,381 C. 46,371 D. 46,381

14. Multiply: 987 14.____
$\underline{867}$
A. 854,609 B. 854,729 C. 855,709 D. 855,729

15. Divide: $59\overline{)321439.0}$ 15.____
A. 5438.1 B. 5447.1 C. 5448.1 D. 5457.1

16. Divide: $.052\overline{)721}$ 16.____
A. 12,648.0 B. 12,648.1 C. 12,649.0 D. 12,649.1

17. If the total number of employees in one city agency increased from 1,927 to 2,006 during a certain year, the percentage increase in the number of employees for that year is MOST NEARLY 17.____
A. 4% B. 5% C. 6% D. 7%

18. During a single fiscal year, which totaled 248 workdays, one account clerk verified 1,488 purchase vouchers. 18.____
Assuming a normal work week of five days, what is the AVERAGE number of vouchers verified by the account clerk in a one-week period during this fiscal year?
A. 25 B. 30 C. 35 D. 40

19. Multiplying a number by .75 is the same as 19.____
A. multiplying it by $^2/_3$
B. dividing it by $^2/_3$
C. multiplying it by ¾
D. dividing it by ¾

20. In City Agency A, $^2/_3$ of the employees are enrolled in a retirement system. City Agency B has the same number of employees as Agency A and 60% of these are enrolled in a retirement system. 20.____
If Agency A has a total of 660 employees, how many MORE employees does it have enrolled in a retirement system than does Agency B?
A. 36 B. 44 C. 56 D. 66

21. Net worth is equal to assets minus liabilities. 21.____
If, at the end of 2019, a textile company had assets of $98,695.83 and liabilities of $59,238.29, what was its net worth?
A. $38,478.54 B. $38,488.64 C. $39,457.54 D. $48,557.54

22. Mr. Martin's assets consist of the following: Cash on hand, $5,233.74, Automobile, $3,206.09; Furniture, $4,925.00; Government Bonds, $5,500.00; and House, $36,69.85. 22.____
What are his TOTAL assets?
A. $54,545.68 B. $54,455.68 C. $55,455.68 D. $55,555.68

23. If Mr. Mitchell has $627.04 in his checking account and then writes three checks for $241.75, $13.24, and $102.97, what will be his new balance? 23.____
A. $257.88 B. $269.08 C. $357.96 D. $369.96

24. An employee's net pay is equal to his total earnings less all deductions. 24.____
If an employee's total earnings in a pay period are $497.05, what is his net pay if he has the following deductions: Federal Income Tax, $18.79; City Tax, $7.25; Pension, $1.88?
A. $351.17 B. $351.07 C. $350.17 D. $350.07

25. A petty cash fund had an opening balance of $85.75 on December 1. Expenditures of $23.00, $15.65, $5.23, $14.75, and $26.38 were made out of this fund during the first 14 days of the month. Then, on December 17, another $38.50 was added to the fund. 25.____
If additional expenditures of $17.18, $3.29, and $11.64 were made during the remainder of the month, what was the FINAL balance of the petty cash fund at the end of December?
A. $6.93 B. $7.13 C. $46.51 D. $91.40

KEY (CORRECT ANSWERS)

1.	B	11.	B
2.	A	12.	B
3.	B	13.	C
4.	A	14.	D
5.	D	15.	C
6.	C	16.	D
7.	C	17.	A
8.	D	18.	B
9.	A	19.	C
10.	B	20.	B

21.	C
22.	D
23.	B
24.	D
25.	B

SOLUTIONS TO PROBLEMS

1. (\$132,000)(.61) – (\$125,500)(.60) = \$5,220

2. Interest = \$1,950. As a percent, \$1950 ÷ 15,000 = 13%

3. New balance = \$253.36 + \$36.95 + \$210.23 + \$7.34 - \$117.35 - \$23.37 - \$15.98 = \$351.18

4. Rent = (\$97,254)(.27) = \$26,258.58

5. (\$2,436.18)(.06) ≈ \$146.17

6. (\$397.50 - \$13.18 - \$122.76) = \$8,631.48

7. (\$14.90)($\frac{18}{2}$) = \$134.10

8. (\$6,500 + \$52,585 + \$35,700 + \$1,275)(1.18) = \$113,350.80

9. (\$710.72 - \$125.44 - \$50.26 - \$12.58 - \$2.54)($\frac{8}{2}$) = \$2,079.60

10. (1 - .34 - .03 - .25 - .36) - \$1,800 = \$107.88

11. (36.69)(52) - \$1,800 = \$107.88

12. \$20,800 – (26)(\$162.84+\$44.26+\$29.72+\$13.94+\$3.14) = \$14,198.60

13. 8,936 + 7,821 + 8,953 + 4,297 + 9,785 + 6,579 = 46,371

14. (987)(867) – 855,729

15. 321,439 ÷ 59 ≈ 5,448.1

16. 721 ÷ .057 ≈ 12,649.1

17. (2,006-1,927) ÷ 1,927 ≈ 4%

18. Let x = number of vouchers. Then, $\frac{x}{5} = \frac{1488}{248}$. Solving, x = 30

19. Multiplying by .75 is equivalent to multiplying by $\frac{3}{4}$

20. (660)($\frac{2}{3}$) – (660)(.60) = 44

21. Net worth = \$98,695.83 - \$59,238.29 = \$39,457.54

22. Total Assets = $5,233.74 + $3,206.09 + $4,925.00 + $5,500.00) + $36,690.85 = $55,555.68.

23. New balance = $627.04 - $241.75 - $13.24 - $102.97 = $269.08

24. Net pay = $497.05 - $90.32 - $28.74 - $18.79 - $7.25 - $1.88 = $350.07

25. Final balance = $85.75 - $23.00 - $15.65 - $5.23 - $14.75 - $26.38 + $38.50 - $17.18 - $3.29 - $11.64 = $7.13

TEST 2

DIRECTIONS: Each question or incomplete statement is followed by several suggested answers or completions. Select the one that BEST answers the question or completes the statement. *PRINT THE LETTER OF THE CORRECT ANSWER IN THE SPACE AT THE RIGHT.*

1. The formula for computing base salary is: Earnings equals base gross plus additional gross. 1.____
If an employee's earnings during a particular period are in the amounts of $597.45, $535.92, $639.91, and $552.83, and his base gross salary is $525.50 per paycheck, what is the TOTAL of the additional gross earned by the employee during that period?
A. $224.11 B. $224.21 C. $224.51 D. $244.11

2. If a lump sum death benefit is paid by the retirement system in an amount equal to 3/7 of an employee's last yearly salary of $13,486.50, the amount of the death benefit paid is MOST NEARLY 2.____
A. $5,749.29 B. $5,759.92 C. $5,779.92 D. $5,977.29

3. Suppose that a member has paid 15 installments on a 28-installment loan. 3.____
The percentage of the number of installments paid to the retirement system is
A. 53.57% B. 53.97% C. 54.57% D. 55.37%

4. If an employee takes a 1-month vacation during a calendar year, the percentage of the year during which he works is MOST NEARLY 4.____
A. 90.9% B. 91.3% C. 91.6% D. 92.1%

5. Suppose that an employee took a leave of absence totaling 7 months during a calendar year. 5.____
Assuming the employee did not take any vacation time during the remainder of that year, the percentage of the year in which he worked is MOST NEARLY
A. 41.7% B. 43.3% C. 46.5% D. 47.1%

6. A member has borrowed $4,725 from her funds in the retirement system. 6.____
If $3,213 has been repaid, the percentage of the loan which is still outstanding is MOST NEARLY
A. 16% B. 32% C. 48% D. 68%

7. If an employee worked only 24 weeks during the year because of illness, the portion of the year he was out of work was MOST NEARLY 7.____
A. 46% B. 48% C. 51% D. 54%

8. If an employee purchased credit for a 16-week period of service which he had prior to rejoining the retirement system, the percentage of a year he purchased credit for was MOST NEARLY 8.____
A. 27.9% B. 28.8% C. 30.7% D. 33.3%

9. If an employee contributes 2/11 of his yearly salary to his pension fund account, the percentage of his yearly salary which he contributes is MOST NEARLY 9.____
A. 17.9% B. 18.2% C. 18.4% D. 19.0%

10. In 2018, the maximum amount of income from which social security tax could be withheld (base salary) was $70,500. In 2020, the base salary was $82,500. The 2020 base salary represents a percentage increase over the 2018 base salary of APPROXIMATELY 10.____
A. 15% B. 16% C. 17% D. 18%

11. If 17.5% of an employee's salary is withheld for taxes, the one of the following which is the fraction of the salary withheld is 11.____
A. 3/20 B. 8/35 C. 7/40 D. 4/25

12. If a person withdraws 42% of the funds from his account with the retirement system, the remaining balance represents a fraction of MOST NEARLY 12.____
A. 7/13 B. 5/9 C. 7/12 D. 4/7

13. A property decreases in value from $45,000 to $35,000. The percent of decrease is MOST NEARLY 13.____
A. 20.5% B. 22.2% C. 25.0% D. 28.6%

14. The fraction $\frac{487}{101326}$ expressed as a decimal is MOST NEARLY 14.____
A. .0482 B. .00481 C. .0049 D. .00392

15. The reciprocal of the sum of 2/3 and 1/6 can be expressed as 15.____
A. 0.83 B. 1.20 C. 1.25 D. 1.50

16. Total land and building costs for a new commercial property equal $50 per square foot.
If the investors expect a 10 percent return on their costs, and if total operating expenses average 5 percent of total costs, annual gross rentals per square foot must be AT LEAST 16.____
A. $7.50 B. $8.50 C. $10.00 D. $12.00

17. The formula for computing the amount of annual deposit in a compound interest bearing account to provide a lump sum at the end of a period of years is $X = \frac{r.L}{(l+r)^{n-1}}$ (X is the amount of annual deposit, r is the rate of interest, and n is the number of years and L = lump sum).
Using the formula, the annual amount of the deposit at the end of each year to accumulate $20,000 at the end of 3 years with interest at 2 percent on annual balances is 17.____
A. $6,120.00 B. $6,203.33 C. $6,535.09 D. $6,666.66

18. An investor sold two properties at $150,000 each. On one he made a 2.5 percent profit. On the other, he suffered a 25 percent loss. 18.____
The NET result of his sales was
A. neither a gain nor a loss
B. a $20,000 loss
C. a $75,000 gain
D. a $75,000 loss

19. A contractor decides to install a chain fence covering the perimeter of a parcel 75 feet wide and 112 feet in depth. 19.____
Which one of the following represents the number of feet to be covered?
A. 187
B. 364
C. 374
D. 8,400

20. A builder estimates he can build an average of 4½ one-family homes to an acre. There are 640 acres to one square mile. 20.____
Which one of the following CORRECTLY represents the number of one-family homes the builder would estimate he can build on one square mile?
A. 1,280
B. 1,920
C. 2,560
D. 2,880

21. $.01059 deposit at 7 percent interest will yield $1.00 in 30 years. 21.____
If a person deposited $1,059 at 7 percent interest on April 4, 1991, which one of the following amounts would represent the worth of this deposit on March 31, 2021?
A. $100
B. $1,000
C. $10,000
D. $100,000

22. A building has an economic life of forty years. 22.____
Assuming the building depreciates at a constant annual rate, which one of the following CORRECTLY represents the yearly percentage of depreciation?
A. 2.0%
B. 2.5%
C. 5.0%
D. 7.0%

23. A building produces a gross income of $200,000 with a net income of $20,000, before mortgage charges and capital recapture. The owner is able to increase the gross income 5 percent without a corresponding increase in operating costs. 23.____
The effect upon the net income will be an INCREASE of
A. 5%
B. 10%
C. 12.5%
D. 50%

24. The present value of $1.00 not payable for 8 years, and at 10 percent interest, is $.4665. 24.____
Which of the following amounts represents the PRESENT value of $1,000 payable 8 years hence at 10 percent interest?
A. $46.65
B. $466.50
C. $4,665.00
D. $46,650.00

25. The amount of real property taxes to be levied by a city is $100 million. The assessment roll subject to taxation shows an assessed valuation of $2 billion. 25.____
Which one of the following tax rates CORRECTLY represents the tax rate to be levied per $100 of assessed valuation?
A. $.50
B. $5.00
C. $50.00
D. $500.00

KEY (CORRECT ANSWERS)

1. A
2. C
3. A
4. C
5. A

6. B
7. D
8. C
9. B
10. C

11. C
12. C
13. B
14. B
15. B

16. A
17. C
18. B
19. C
20. D

21. D
22. B
23. D
24. B
25. B

SOLUTIONS TO PROBLEMS

1. \$597.45 + \$535.91 + \$639.91 + \$552.83 = \$2,326.11. Then, \$2,326.11 – (4)(\$525.50) = \$224.11

2. Death benefit = (\$13,486.50)($\frac{3}{7}$) ≈ \$5,779.92

3. $\frac{15}{28}$ ≈ 53.57%

4. $\frac{11}{12}$ ≈ 91.6% (closer to 91.7%)

5. $\frac{5}{12}$ ≈ 41.7%

6. (\$4,725-\$3,213) ÷ \$4,725 = 32%

7. $\frac{28}{52}$ ≈ 54%

8. $\frac{16}{52}$ ≈ 30.7% (closer to 30.8%)

9. $\frac{2}{11}$ ≈ 18.2%

10. (\$82,500 - \$70,500) ÷ \$70,500 = 17%

11. 17.5% = $\frac{175}{1000}$ = $\frac{7}{40}$

12. 100% - 42% = 58% = $\frac{58}{100}$ = $\frac{29}{50}$, closest to $\frac{7}{12}$ in selections

13. $\frac{\$10,000}{\$45,000}$ ≈ 22.2%

14. 487/101,216 ≈ .00481

15. $\frac{2}{3}+\frac{1}{6}=\frac{5}{6}$ Then, $1 \div \frac{5}{6}=\frac{6}{5}$ = 1.20

16. (.15)(\$50) = \$7.50

17. x = (.02)(\$20,000)/[(1+.02)^3 – 1] = 400 ÷ .061208 ≈ \$6,535.09

18. Sold 150,000, 25% loss = paid 200,000, loss of \$50,000 Sold 150,000, 25% profit = paid 120,000, profit of 30,000 – 50,000 + 30,000 = 20,000 (loss)

19. Perimeter = (2)(75) + (2)(112) = 374 ft.

20. (640)(4½) = 2,880 homes

21. (1÷.01059)(1059) = $100,000

22. 1÷4 = .025 = 2.5%

23. New gross income = ($200,000)(X1.05) = $210,000
Then, ($210,000-$200,000) ÷ $20,000 = 50%

24. Let x = present value of $1,000. Then, $\frac{\$1.00}{\$.4665} = \frac{\$1000}{x}$
Solving, x = $466.50

25. Let x = tax rate. Then, $\frac{\$100,000,000}{\$2,000,000,000} = \frac{x}{\$100}$
Solving, x = $5.00

TEST 3

DIRECTIONS: Each question or incomplete statement is followed by several suggested answers or completions. Select the one that BEST answers the question or completes the statement. *PRINT THE LETTER OF THE CORRECT ANSWER IN THE SPACE AT THE RIGHT.*

1. It is found that for the past three years the average weekly number of inspections per inspector ranged from 20 inspections to 40 inspections. 1.____
On the basis of this information, it is MOST reasonable to conclude that
   A. on the average, 30 inspections per week were made
   B. the average weekly number of inspections never fell below 20
   C. the performance of inspectors deteriorated over the three-year period
   D. the range in average weekly inspections was 60

Questions 2-4.

DIRECTIONS: Questions 2 through 4 are to be answered on the basis of the following information.

The number of students admitted to University X in 2019 from High School Y was 268 students. This represented 13.7 percent of University X's entering freshman classes. In 2020, it is expected that University X will admit 591 students from High School Y, which is expected to represent 19.4 percent of the 2020 entering freshman classes of University X.

2. Which of the following is CLOSEST estimate of the size of University's expected 2020 entering freshman classes? 2.____
_____ students
   A. 2,000   B. 2,500   C. 3,000   D. 3,500

3. Of the following, the expected percentage of increase from 2019 to 2020 in the number of students graduating from High School Y and entering University X as freshmen is MOST NEARLY 3.____
   A. 5.7%   B. 20%   C. 45%   D. 120%

4. Assume that the cost of processing admission to University X from High School Y in 2019 was an average of $28. Also, that this was 1/3 more than the average cost of processing each of the other 2019 freshmen admissions to University X. 4.____
Then, the one of the following that MOST closely shows the total processing cost of all 2019 freshman admissions to University X is
   A. $6,500   B. $20,000   C. $30,000   D. $40,000

5. Assume that during the fiscal year 2019-2020, a bureau produced 20% more work units than it produced in the fiscal year 2018-2019. Also assume that during the fiscal year 2019-2020 that bureau's staff was 20% smaller than it was in the fiscal year 2018-2019. 5.____

On the basis of this information, it would be MOST proper to conclude that the number of work units produced per staff member in that bureau in the fiscal year 2019-2020 exceeded the number of work units produced per staff member in that bureau in the fiscal year 2018-2019 by which one of the following percentages?

A. 20% B. 25% C. 40% D. 50%

6. Assume that during the following fiscal years (FY), a bureau has received the following appropriations: 6.____

FY 2015-2016 - $200,000
FY 2016-2017 - $240,000
FY 2017-2018 - $280,000
FY 2018-2019 - $390,000
FY 2019-2020 - $505,000

The bureau's appropriation for which one of the following fiscal years showed the LARGEST percentage of increase over the bureau's appropriation for the immediately previous fiscal year?

A. FY 2016-2017 B. FY 2017-2018
C. FY 2018-2019 D. FY 2010-2020

7. Assume that the number of buses (U_t) required for a given line-haul system serving the Central Business District depends upon roundtrip time (t), capacity of bus (c), and the total number of people to be moved in a peak hour (P) in the major direction, i.e., in the morning and out in the evening. 7.____

The formula for the number of buses required is U_t =

A. Ptc B. $\frac{tP}{c}$ C. $\frac{cP}{t}$ D. $\frac{ct}{P}$

8. The area, in blocks, that can be served by a single stop for any maximum walking distance is given by the following formula: $a = 2w^2$. In this formula, a = the area served by a stop and w = maximum walking distance. 8.____

If people will tolerate a walk of up to three blocks, how many stops would be needed to service an area of 288 square blocks?

A. 9 B. 16 C. 18 D. 27

Questions 9-11.

DIRECTIONS: Questions 9 through 11 are to be answered on the basis of the following information.

In 2019, a police precinct records 456 cases of car thefts, which is 22.6 percent of all grand larcenies. In 2020, there were 560 such cases, which constituted 35% of the broader category.

9. The number of crimes in the broader category in 2020 was MOST NEARLY 9.____

A. 1,600 B. 1,700 C. 1,960 D. 2,800

10. The change from 2019 to 2020 in the number of crimes in the broader category represented MOST NEARLY a 10.____
    A. 2.5% decrease B. 10.1% increase
    C. 12.5% increase D. 20% decrease

11. In 2020, one out of every 6 of these crimes was solved. 11.____
    This represents MOST NEARLY what percentage of the total number of crimes in the broader category that year?
    A. 5.8 B. 6 C. 9.3 D. 12

12. Assume that a maintenance shop does 5 brake jobs to every 3 front-end jobs. It does 8,000 jobs altogether in a 240-day year. In one day, one worker can do 3 front-end jobs or 4 brake jobs. 12.____
    About how many workers will be needed in the shop?
    A. 3 B. 5 C. 10 D. 18

13. Assume that the price of a certain item declines by 6% one year, and then increases by 5 and 10 percent, respectively, during the next two years. 13.____
    What is the OVERALL increase in price over the three-year period?
    A. 4.2 B. 6 C. 8.6 D. 10.1

14. After finding the total percent change in a price (TO) over a three-year period, as in the preceding question, one could compute the average annual percent change in the price by using the formula 14.____
    A. $(1+TC)^{1/3}$ B. $\frac{(1+TC)}{3}$ C. $(1+TC)^{1/3-1}$ D. $\frac{1}{(1+TC)^{1/3}-1}$

15. 357 is 6% of 15.____
    A. 2,142 B. 5,950 C. 4,140 D. 5,900

16. In 2019, a department bought n pieces of a certain supply item for a total of \$x. In 2020, the department bought k percent fewer of the item but had to pay a total of g percent more for it. 16.____
    Which of the following formulas is CORRECT for determining the average price per item in 2020?
    A. $100\frac{xg}{nk}$ B. $\frac{x(100+g)}{n(100-k)}$ C. $\frac{x(100-g)}{n(100+k)}$ D. $\frac{x}{n}$ - $100\frac{g}{k}$

17. A sample of 18 income tax returns, each with 4 personal exemptions, is taken for 2019 and 2020. The breakdown is as follows in terms of income: 17.____

Average Gross Income (in thousands)	Number of Returns	
	2019	2020
40	6	2
80	10	11
120	2	5

There is a personal deduction per exemption of \$500.
There are no other expense deductions. In addition, there is an exclusion of \$3,000 for incomes less than \$50,000 and \$2,000 for incomes from \$50,000 to \$99,999.99. From \$100,000 upward there is no exclusion.

The average net taxable income for the samples in thousands for 2019 is MOST NEARLY
A. $67 B. $85 C. $10 D. $128

18. In the preceding question, the increase in average net taxable income for the sample (in thousands) between 2019 and 2020 is 18.____
A. 16 B. 20 C. 24 D. 34

19. Assume that supervisor S has four subordinates—A, B, C, and D. 19.____
The MAXIMUM number of relationships, assuming that all combinations are included, that can exist between S and his subordinates is
A. 28 B. 15 C. 7 D. 4

20. If the workmen's compensation insurance rate for clerical workers is 93 cents per $100 of wages, the total premium paid by a city whose clerical staff earns $8,765,000 is MOST NEARLY 20.____
A. $8,150 B. $81,515 C. $87,650 D. $93,765

21. Assume that a budget of $3,240,000,000 for the fiscal year beginning July 1, 2020 has been approved. A city sales tax is expected to provide $1,100,000,000; licenses, fees and sundry revenues ae expected to yield $121,600,000; the balance is to be raised from property taxes. A tax equalization board has appraised all property in the city at a fair value of $42,500,000,000. The council wishes to assess property at 60% of its fair value. 21.____
The tax rate would need to be MOST NEARLY _____ per $100 of assessed value.
A. $12.70 B. $10.65 C. $7.90 D. $4.00

22. Men's white linen handkerchiefs cost $12.90 for 3. 22.____
The cost per dozen handkerchiefs is
A. $77.40 B. $38.70 C. $144.80 D. $51.60

23. Assume that it is necessary to partition a room measuring 40 feet by 20 feet into eight smaller rooms of equal size. 23.____
Allowing no room for aisles, the MINIMUM amount of partitioning that would be needed is _____ feet.
A. 90 B. 100 C. 110 D. 140

24. Assume that two types of files have been ordered: 200 of type A and 100 of type B. When the files are delivered, the buyer discovers that 25% of each type is damaged. Of the remaining files, 20% of type A and 40% of type B are the wrong color. 24.____
The total number of files that are the WRONG COLOR is
A. 30 B. 40 C. 50 D. 60

25. In a unit of five inspectors, one inspector makes an average of 12 inspections a day, two inspectors make an average of 10 inspections a day, and two inspectors make an average of 9 inspections a day. 25.____
If in a certain week one of the inspectors who makes an average of nine inspections a day is out of work on Monday and Tuesday because of illness and all the inspectors do no inspections for half a day on Wednesday because of a special meeting, the number of inspections this unit can be expected to make in that week is MOST NEARLY
A. 215 B. 225 C. 230 D. 250

KEY (CORRECT ANSWERS)

1. B
2. C
3. D
4. D
5. D

6. C
7. B
8. B
9. A
10. D

11. A
12. C
13. C
14. C
15. B

16. B
17. A
18. A
19. B
20. B

21. C
22. D
23. B
24. D
25. A

SOLUTIONS TO PROBLEMS

1. Since the number of weekly inspections ranged from 20 to 40, this implies that the average weekly number of inspections never fell below 20.

2. 591 ÷ 194 ≈ 3046, closest to 3,000 students

3. (591-268) ÷ 268 = 120%

4. Total processing cost = (268)(28) + (1,688)($21) = $42,952, closest to $40,000. [Note: Since 268 represents 13.7%, total freshman population = 268 ÷ .137 ≈ 1,956. Then, 1,956 – 268 = 1,688]

5. Let x = staff size in 2018-2019. Then, .80x = staff size in 2019-2020. Since the 2019-2020 staff produced 20% more work, this is represented by 1.20. However, to measure the productivity per staff member, the factor 1/.80 = 1.25 must also be used to equate the 2 staffs. Then, (1.20)(1.25) = 1.50. Thus, the 2019-2020 staff produced 50% more than the 2018-2019 staff.

6. The respective percent increases are ≈ 20%, 17%, 39%, 29%. The largest would be, over the previous fiscal year, for the current fiscal year 2018-2019

7. $\frac{P}{c}$ = number of buses needed per hour. If t = time (in hrs.), then U_t = tP.c

8. a = (2)(9) = 18 for 1 stop. Then, 288 ÷ 18 = 15 stops.

9. 560 ÷ .35 = 1600 grand larcenies.

10. 456 ÷ .226 = 2018; 560 ÷ .35 = 1600. Then, (1,600-2,018) ÷ 2,018 = -20% or a 20% decrease.

11. $(\frac{1}{6})(560) = 93\frac{1}{3}$. Then, $93\frac{1}{3}$ ÷ 1,600 = 5.8%

12. There are 5,000 brake jobs and 3,000 front-end jobs in one year.
5,000 ÷ 4 = 1,250 days, and 1,250 ÷ 240 ≈ 5.2. Also, 3,000 ÷ 3 = 1,000 days, and 1,000 ÷ 240 ≈ 4.2. Total number of workers needed ≈ 5.2 + 4.2 ≈ 10.

13. (.94)(1.05)(1.10) = 1.0857, which represents an overall increase by about 8.6%.

14. Average annual % change = $(1+TC)^{1/3} - 1 = (1.0857)^{1/3} - 1 \approx 2.8\%$.

15. 357 ÷ .06 = 5,950

16. In 2020, $(h)(1-\frac{k}{100})$ pieces cost $(x)(1+\frac{g}{100})$ dollars. To calculate the cost for 1 piece (average cost), find the value of $[(x)(1+\frac{G}{100})] \div [(n)(1-\frac{K}{100})]$ = [(x)(100+g)/100]. [100/{n(100-k)}] = [x(100+g)]/[n(100-k)

17.

	#	Deductions Up to 50,000	
40,000	6	2000 3000	40,000-3,000-2,000 = 35,000 x 6
80,000	10	2000 2000	80,000-2,000-2,000 = 76,000 x 10
20,000	2	2000	= 118000 x 2

35,000 x 6 = 210,000 = 210
76,000 x 10 = 760,000 = 760
118,800 x 2 = 236,000 = 236
1206

1206 ÷ 18 = 67

18.

2020		Deductions		
40,000	2	2000 3000	35,000 x 2 =	70,000
80,000	11	2000 2000	76,000 x 11 =	836,000
120,000	5	2000	118,000 x 5 =	590,000
				1,496,000

1,496,000/18 = 83,111
83,111 – 67,000 = 16,111 = most nearly 16 (in thousands)

19. We are actually looking for the number of different groups of different sizes involving S. This reduces to ${}_4C_1 + {}_4C_2 + {}_4C_2 + {}_4C_4 = 4 + 6 + 4 + 1 = 15$. The notation ${}_nC_r$ means combinations of n things taken R at a time = [(n)(n-1)(n-2)(...)(n-R+1)]/[(R)(R-1)(...)(1)]. The 15 groups are: SA, SB, SC, SD, SAB, SAC, SAD, SBC, SBD, SCD, SABC, SABD, SACD, SBCD, SABCD.

20. Let x = total premiums. Then, $\frac{.93}{100} = \frac{X}{8,765,000}$ Solving, x = $81,515

21. The balance, raised from property taxes, = $3,240,000,000 - $1,100,000,000 – $121,600,000 = $2,018,400,000. Now, (.60)($42,500,000,000) = $25,500,000. The tax rate per $100 of assessed value = ($2,018,400,000)($100)(/$25,500,000,00 = $7.90.

22. A dozen costs ($12.90)($\frac{12}{3}$) = $51.60.

23. (40(20) ÷ 8 = 100 ft.

24. Total number of wrong-color files = (200)(.75)(.20)+(100)(.75)(.40) = 60

25. Weekly number of inspections = (12×5) + (10×5) + (10×5) + (9×5) + 9×5) = 250
Subtract: 9 Monday, 9 Tuesday, 25 Wednesday
Total: 250 – 9 – 9 – 25 = 207
Closest entry is choice A.

BASIC FUNDAMENTALS OF BOOKKEEPING

CONTENTS

BASIC FUNDAMENTALS OF BOOKKEEPING

I. INTRODUCTION

Why keep records? If you are a typical small-business man, your answer to this question is probably, "Because the Government requires it!" And if the question comes in the middle of a busy day, you may add a few heartfelt words about the amount of time you have to spend on records--just for the Government.

Is it "just for the Government," though? True, regulations of various governmental agencies have greatly increased the record-keeping requirements of business. But this may be a good thing for the small-business man, overburdened though he is.

Many small-business managers don't recognize their bookkeeping records for what they can really do. Their attitudes concerning these records are typified by one businessman who said, "Records only tell you what you have done in the past. It's too late to do anything about the past; I need to know what is going to happen in the future. "However, the past can tell us much about what may happen in the future; and, certainly we can profit in the future from knowledge of our past mistakes.

These same managers may recognize that records are necessary in filing their tax returns, or that a banker requires financial information before he will lend money, but often their appreciation of their bookkeeping systems ends at this point. However, there are many ways in which the use of such information can help an owner manage his business more easily and profitably.

The small-businessman is confronted with an endless array of problems and decisions every day. Sound decisions require an informed manager; and many management problems can be solved with the aid of the right bookkeeping information.

II. REQUIREMENTS OF A GOOD RECORD SYSTEM

Of course, to get information that is really valuable to you--to get the right information--requires a good bookkeeping system. What are the characteristics of a good system? You want one that is simple and easy to understand, reliable, accurate, consistent, and one that will get the information to you promptly.

A simple, well-organized system of records, regularly kept up, can actually be a timesaver--by bringing order out of disorder. Furthermore, competition is very strong in today's business areas. A businessman needs to know almost on a day-to-day basis where his business stands profit wise, which lines of merchandise or services are the most or the least profitable, what his working-capital needs are, and many other details. He can get this information with reasonable certainty only if he has a good recordkeeping system—one that gives him all the information he needs.

In setting up a recordkeeping system that is tailored to your business, you will probably need the professional help of a competent accountant. And you may want to retain the services of an accountant or bookkeeper to maintain these records. But it is your job to learn to interpret this information and to use it effectively.

One of the reasons that many managers have misgivings about keeping records is that they don't understand them or know how they can be used. The owner or manager of a small business may be an expert in his line of business; however, he generally does not have a background in keeping records. So he is usually confused. What we will try to do in this discussion is to highlight the "why and what of bookkeeping." In so-doing, we aim to eliminate that confusion.

III. IMPORTANT BOOKKEEPING RECORDS

Today's managers should be familiar with the following bookkeeping records:

- Journal
- Ledgers
- Balance sheet
- Income statement
- Funds flow statement

We will discuss each of them in turn. In addition, a brief discussion of other supporting records will be made.

A. Bookkeeping Books

The journal, which accountants call "the book of original entry," is a chronological record of all business transactions engaged in by the firm. It is simply a financial diary. The ledgers, or "books of account," are more specialized records used to classify the journal entries according to like elements. For example, there would be a separate ledger account for cash entries, another for all sales, and still others for items such as accounts receivable, inventory, and loans. All transactions are first entered in the journal, and then posted in the appropriate ledger. The journal and ledgers are of minor importance to the manager in making decisions, but they play a vital role for the accountant or bookkeeper because the more important accounting statements such as the balance sheet and the income statement are derived from the journal and ledger entries.

B. Financial Reports

The two principal financial reports in most businesses are the balance sheet and the income statement. Up to about 25 or 30 years ago, the balance sheet was generally considered to be the most important financial statement. Until that time, it was generally used only as a basis for the extension of credit and bank loans, and very little thought was given to the information it offered that might be important in „the operation and management of the business. Starting about 30 years ago, emphasis has gradually shifted to the income statement. Today the balance sheet and income statements are of equal importance, both to the accountant in financial reporting and to the manager faced with a multitude of administrative problems.

Essentially, the balance sheet shows what a business has, what it owes, and the investment of the owners in the business. It can be likened to a snapshot, showing the financial condition of the business *at a certain point in time.* The income statement, on the other hand, is a summary of business operations for a certain period--usually between two balance sheet dates. The income statement can be compared to a moving picture; it indicates the activity of a business *over a certain period of time.* In very general terms, the balance sheet tells you where you are, and the income statement tells you how you got there since the last time you had a balance sheet prepared.

Both the balance sheet and income statement can be long and complicated documents. Both accountants and management need some device that can highlight the critical financial information contained in these complex documents. Certain standard ratios or relationships between items on the financial statements have been developed that allow the interested parties to quickly determine important characteristics of the firm's activities. There are many relationships that might be important in a specific business that would not be as significant in another.

Other devices of the bookkeeper, such as funds flow statements, daily summaries of sales and cash receipts, the checkbook, account receivable records, property depreciation records, and insurance scheduling have also been found useful to management.

C. The Balance Sheet

As stated earlier, the balance sheet represents what a business has, what it owes, and the investment of the owners. The things of value that the business has or owns are called *assets*. The claims of creditors against these assets are called liabilities. The value of the assets over and above the *liabilities* can be justifiably called the owner's claim. This amount is usually called the owner's equity (or net worth).

This brings us to the *dual-aspect concept* of bookkeeping. The balance sheet is set up to portray two aspects of each entry or event recorded on it. For each thing of value, or asset, there is a claim against that asset. The recognition of this concept leads to the balance sheet formula: ASSETS = LIABILITIES + OWNER'S EQUITY. Let's take an example to clarify this concept. Suppose Joe Smith decides to start a business. He has $2,000 cash in the bank. He got this sum by investing $1,000 of his own money and by borrowing $1,000 from the bank. If he were to draw up a balance sheet at this time, he would have assets of $2 000 cash balanced against a liability claim of $1,000 and an owner's claim of $1,000. Using the balance sheet formula: $2,000 = $1,000 + $1,000. This formula means there will always be a balance between assets and claims against them. The balance sheet *always* balances unless there has been a clerical error.

The balance sheet is usually, constructed in a two-column format. The assets appear in the left hand column and the claims against the assets (the liabilities and owner's equity) are in the right hand column. Other formats are sometimes used; but, in any case, the balance sheet is-an itemized or detailed account of the basic formula: as sets = liabilities + owner's equity.

1. Assets

I have been speaking of assets belonging to the business. Of course, the business does not legally own anything unless it is organized as a corporation. But regardless of whether the business is organized as a proprietorship, a partnership, or a corporation, all business book-keeping should be reckoned and accounted apart from the accounting of the personal funds and assets of, its owners.

Assets are typically classified into three categories:

- Current assets
- Fixed assets
- Other assets

a. Current Assets

For bookkeeping purposes, the term "current assets" is used to designate cash and other assets which can be converted to cash during the normal operating cycle of the business (usually one year). The distinction between current assets and noncurrent assets is important since lenders and others pay much attention to the total amount of current assets. The size of current assets has a significant relationship to the stability of the business because it represents, to some degree, the amount of cash that might be raised quickly to meet current obligations. Here are some of the major current asset items.

Cash consists of funds that are immediately available to use without restrictions. These funds are usually in the form of checking-account deposits in banks, cash-register money, and petty cash. Cash should be large enough to meet obligations that are immediately due.

Accounts, receivable are Arricnint8 'Owed to the company by its customers as a result of sales. Essentially, these accounts are the result of granting credit to customers. They may take the form of charge accounts where no interest or service charge is made, or they may be of an interest-bearing nature. In either case they are a drain on working capital. The more that is outstanding on accounts receivable, the less money that is available to meet current needs. The trick with accounts receivable is to keep them small enough so as not to endanger working capital, but large enough to keep from losing sales to credit-minded customers.

Inventory is defined as those items which are held for sale in the ordinary course of business, or which are to be consumed in the production of goods and services that are to be sold. Since accountants are conservative by nature, they include in inventory only items that are salable, and these items are valued at cost or market value, whichever is lower? Control of inventory and inventory expenses is one of management's most important jobs-particularly for retailers--and good bookkeeping records in this area are particularly useful.

Prepaid expenses represent assets, paid for in advance, but whose usefulness will usually expire in a short time. A good example of this is prepaid insurance. A business pays for insurance protection in advance--usually three to five years in advance. The right to this protection is a thing of value--an asset--and the unused portion can be refunded or converted to cash.

b. Fixed Assets

"Fixed assets" are items owned by the business that have relatively long life. These assets are used in the production or sale of other goods and services. If they were held for resale, they would be classified as inventory, even though they might be long-lived assets.

Normally these assets are composed of land, buildings, and equipment. Some companies lump their fixed assets into one entry on their balance sheets, but you gain more information and can exercise more control over these assets if they are listed separately on the balance sheet. You may even want to list various types of equipment separately.

There is one other aspect of fixed-asset bookkeeping that we should discuss--and this is depreciation. Generally fixed assets-with the exception of land-depreciate, or decrease in value with the passing of time. That is, a building or piece of equipment that is five years old is not worth as much as it was when it was new. For a balance sheet to show the true value of these assets, it must reflect this loss in value. For both tax and other accounting purposes, the businessman is allowed to deduct this loss in value each year over the useful life of the assets, until, over a period of time, he has deducted the total cost of the asset. There are several accepted ways to calculate how much of an asset's value can be deducted for depreciation in a given year. Depreciation is allowed as an expense item on the income statement, and we will discuss this fact later.

c. Other Assets

"Other assets" is a miscellaneous category. It accounts for any investments of the firm in securities, such as stock in other private companies or government bonds. It also includes intangible assets such as goodwill, patents, and franchise costs. Items in the "other-assets" category have a longer life than current-asset items.

2. Liabilities

"Liabilities" are the amounts of money owed by the business to people other than the owners. They are claims against the company's total assets, although they are not claims against any specific asset, except in the cases of some mortgages and equipment liens. Essentially, liabilities are divided into two classes:

Current liabilities

Long-term Liabilities

a. Current Liabilities

The term "current liabilities" is used to describe those claims of outsiders on the business that will fall, due within one year. Here are some of the more important current-liabilities entries on the balance sheet:

Accounts payable represent the amounts owed to vendors, wholesalers, and other suppliers from whom the business has bought items on account. This includes any items of inventory, supply, or capital equipment which have been purchased on credit and for which payment is expected in less than one year. For example, a retail butcher purchased 500 pounds of meat for $250, a quantity of fish that cost $50, and a new air-conditioning unit for his store for $450. He bought all of these items on 60-day terms. His accounts payable were increased by $750. Of course, at the same time his inventory increased by $300 and his fixed assets rose by $450. If he had paid cash for these items, his accounts payable would not have been affected, but his cash account would have decreased by $750, thus keeping the accounting equation in balance.

Short-term loans, which are sometimes called notes payable, are loans from individuals, banks, or other lending institutions which fall due within a year. Also included in this category is the portion of any long-term debt that will come due within a year.

Accrued expenses are obligations which the company has incurred, but for 'which there has been no formal bill or invoice as yet. An example of this is accrued taxes. The owner knows the business has the obligation to pay taxes; and they are accruing or accumulating each day. The fact that the taxes do not have to be paid until a later date does not diminish the obligation. Another example of accrued expenses is wages. Although wages are paid weekly or monthly, they are being earned hourly or daily and constitute a valid claim against the company. An accurate balance sheet will reflect these obligations.

b. Long-Term Liabilities

Claims of outsiders on the business that do not come due within one year are called "long-term liabilities" or, simply, "other liabilities." Included in this category are bonded indebtedness, mortgages, and long-term loans from individuals, banks, and others from whom the business may borrow money, such as the SBA. As was stated before, any part of a long-term debt that falls due within one year from the date of the balance sheet would be recorded as part of the current liabilities of the business.

Owner's Equity

The owner's equity section of the balance sheet is located on the right-hand side underneath the listing of the liabilities. It shows the claims of the owners on the company. Essentially, this is a balancing figure--that is, the owners get what's left of the assets after the liability claims have been recognized. This is an obvious definition, if you will remember the balance sheet formula. Transposing the formula as we learned it a few minutes ago, it becomes Assets - Liabilities = Owner's Equity. In the case where the business is a sole proprietorship, it is customary to show owner's equity as one entry with no distinction being made between the owner's initial investment and the accumulated retained earnings of the business. However, in the case of an incorporated business, there are entries for stockholders' claims as well as for earnings that have been accumulated and retained in the business. Of course, if the business has been consistently operating at a loss, the proprietor's claim may be less than his initial investment. And, in the case of a corporation, the balancing account could be operating deficit rather than retained earnings.

If we put together the entries we have been talking about, we have a complete balance sheet. There is a lot of information in this statement. It tells you just what you have and where it is. It also tells you what you owe. You need this information to help you decide what actions you should take in running your business. If you need to borrow money, the banker or anyone else from whom you borrow will want to look at your balance sheet.

D. THE INCOME STATEMENT

In recent years the income statement has become as important as the balance sheet as a financial and management record. It is also called the profit and loss statement, or simply the P and L statement. This financial record summarizes the activities of the company over a period of time, listing those that can be expressed in dollars. That is, it reports the revenues of the company and the expenses incurred in. obtaining the revenues, and it shows the profit or loss resulting from these activities. The income statement complements the balance sheet. While balance sheet analysis shows the change in position of the company at the end of accounting periods, the income statement shows how the change took place during the accounting period. Both reports 'are necessary for a full understanding of the operation of the business.

The income statement for particular company should be tailored to fit the activities of that company, and there is no rigid format that must be followed in constructing this report. But the following categories are found in most income statements.

1. Sales

The major activity of most businesses is the sales of products and services, and the bulk of revenue comes from sales. In recording sales, the figure used is net sales-that is, sales after discounts, allowances, and returned goods have been accounted for.

2. Cost of Goods Sold

Another important item, in calculating profit or loss, is the cost of the goods that the company has sold. This item is difficult to calculate accurately. Since the goods sold come from inventory, and since the company may have bought parts of its inventory at several prices, it is hard to determine exactly what is the cost of the particular part of the inventory that was sold. In large companies, and particularly in companies using cost accounting, there are some rather complicated methods of determining "cost of goods sold, " but they are beyond the scope of this presentation. However, there is a simple, generally accepted way of calculating cost of goods sold. In this method you simply add the net amount of purchases during the accounting period to your beginning inventory, and subtract from this your ending inventory. The result can be considered cost-of-goods sold.

3. Gross Margin

The difference between sales and cost of goods sold is called the "gross margin" or gross profit. This item is often expressed as a percentage of sales, as well as in dollar figures. The percentage gross margin is a very significant figure because it indicates what the average markup is on the merchandise sold. So, if a manager knows his expenses as a percentage of sales, he can calculate the mark up necessary to obtain the gross margin he needs for a profitable operation. It is surprising how many small-business men do not know what basis to use in setting markups. In fact, with the various, allowances, discounts, and markdowns that a business may offer, many managers do not know what their markup actually is. The gross margin calculation on the income statement can help the manager with this problem.

There are other costs of running a business besides the cost of the goods sold. When you use the simple method of determining costs of goods sold, these costs are called "expenses."

For example, here are some typical expenses: salaries and wages, utilities, depreciation, interest, administrative expenses, supplies, bad debts, advertising, and taxes--Federal, State, and local. These are typical expenses, but there are many other kinds of expenses that may be experienced by other businesses. For example, we have shown in the Blank Company's balance sheet that he owns his own land and building--with a mortgage, of course. These accounts for part of his depreciation and interest expenses, but for a company that rents its quarters, rent would appear as the expense item. Other common expenses are traveling expense, commissions, and advertising.

Most of these expense items are self-explanatory, but there are a few that merit further comment. For one thing, the salary or draw of the owner should be recorded among the expenses--either as a part of salaries and wages or as part of administrative expenses. To exclude the owner's compensation from expenses distorts the actual profitability of the business. And, if the company is incorporated, it would reduce the allowable tax deductions of the business. Of course, for tax purposes, the owner's salary or draw in a proprietorship or partnership is considered as part of the net profit.

We discussed depreciation when we examined the balance sheet, and we mentioned that it was an item of expense. Although no money is actually paid out for depreciation, it is a real expense because it represents reduction in the value of the assets.

The most important thing about expenses is to be sure to include all of the expenses that the business incurs. This not only helps the owner get a more accurate picture of his operation but it allows him to take full advantage of the tax deductions that legitimate expenses offer.

4. Net Profit

In a typical company when expenses are subtracted from gross margin, the remainder is profit. However, if the business receives revenue from sources other than sales, such as rents, dividends on securities held by the company, or interest on money loaned by the company, it is added to profit at this point. For bookkeeping purposes, the resulting profit is labeled "profit before taxes." This is the figure from which Federal income taxes are figured. If the business is a proprietorship, the profit is taxed as part of the owner's income. If the business is a corporation, the profits may be taxed on the basis of the corporate income tax schedule. When income taxes have been accounted for, the resultant entry is called "net profit after taxes," or simply "net profit." This is usually the final entry on the income statement.

Another financial record which managers can use to advantage is the funds flow statement. This statement is also called statement of sources and uses of funds and sometimes the "where got--where gone" statement. Whatever you call it, a record of sources and uses of past funds is useful to the manager. He can use it to evaluate past performance, and as a guide in determining future uses and sources of money.

When we speak of "funds" we do not necessarily mean actual "dollars" or "cash." Although accounting records are all written in monetary terms, they do not always involve an exchange of money. Many times in business transactions, it is credit rather than dollars that changes hands. Therefore, when we speak of funds flow, we are speaking of exchanges of *economic values* rather than merely the physical flow of dollars.

Basically, funds are used to: increase assets and reduce liabilities. They are also sometimes used to reduce owner's equity. An example of this would be the use of company funds to buy up outstanding stock or to buy out a partner. Where do funds come from? The three basic sources of funds are a reduction in assets, increases in liabilities, and increased owner's equity. All balance sheet items can be affected by the obtaining and spending of company fund's.

To examine the construction and use of a funds flow statement, let's take another look at the Blank Company. Here we show comparative balance sheets for two one-year periods. For the sake of simplicity, we have included only selected items from the balance sheets for analysis. Notice that the company gained funds by:

reducing cash $300,

increasing accounts payable $400,

putting $500 more owner's equity in the business, and

plowing back $800 of the profit into the business.

These funds were used to:

increase accounts receivable $300,
increase inventory $200,

buy $500 worth of equipment, and

pay off $1, 000 worth of long-term debt.

This funds flow statement has indicated to Mr. Blank where he has gotten his funds and how he has spent them. He can analyze these figures in the light of his plans and objectives and take appropriate action.

For example, if Mr. Blank wants to answer the question "Should I buy new capital equipment?" a look at his funds flow statement would show him his previous sources of funds, and it would give him a clue as to whether he could obtain funds for any new equipment.

I V. OTHER RECORDS

Up to this point, we have been talking about the basic types of bookkeeping records. In addition, we have discussed the two basic financial statements of a business: the balance sheet and the profit and loss statement. Now let us give our attention briefly to some other records which are very helpful to running a business successfully.

One element that appears on the balance sheet which I believe we can agree is important is cash. Because it is the lifeblood of all business, cash should be controlled and safeguarded at all times. The daily summary of sales and cash receipts and the checkbook are used by many manager s of small businesses to help provide that control.

A. Daily Summary of Sales and Cash. Receipts

Not all businesses summarize their daily transactions. However, a daily summary of sales and cash receipts is a very useful tool for checking how your business is doing on a day-to-day basis. At the close of each day's business, the actual cash on hand is counted and "balanced" against the total of the receipts recorded for the day. This balancing is done by means of the Daily Summary of Sales and Cash Receipts. This is a recording of every cash 'receipt and every charge sale, whether you use a cash register or sales checks or both. If you have more than one cash register, a daily summary should be prepared for each; the individual cash-register summaries can then be combined into one overall summary for convenience in handling.

In the daily summary form used for purposes of illustration, (see Handout), the first section, "Cash Receipts," records the total of all cash taken in during the day from whatever source. This is the cash that must be accounted for over and above, the amount in the change and/ or petty cash funds. We shall touch upon these two funds later. The three components of cash receipts are (1) cash sales, (2) collections on accounts, and (3) miscellaneous receipts.

The daily total of cash sales is obtained from a cash-register tape reading or, if no cash register is used, by totaling the cash-sales checks.

For collections on accounts, an individual record of each customer payment on account should be kept, whether or not these collections are rung up on a cash register. The amount to be entered on the daily summary is obtained by totaling these individual records.

Miscellaneous receipts are daily cash transactions that cannot be classified as sales or collections. They might include refunds from suppliers for overpayment, advertising rebates or allowances, . collections of rent from sub-leases or concessions, etc. Like collections on account, a sales check or memo should be made out each time such cash is taken in.

The total of daily cash receipts to be accounted for on the daily summary is obtained by adding cash sales, collections on account, and miscellaneous receipts.

The second section, "Cash on Hand," of a daily summary is a count of the cash actually on hand plus the cash that is represented by petty cash slips. The daily summary provides for counts of your total coins, bills, and checks as well as the amount expended for petty cash. The latter is determined by adding the amounts on the individual petty cash slips. By totaling all four of these counts, you obtain the total cash accounted for. To determine the amount of your daily cash deposit, you deduct from the "total cash accounted for" the total of the petty cash and change funds.

Cash to be deposited on the daily summary should always equal the total receipts to be accounted for minus the fixed amount of your petty cash and change funds. If it does not, all the work in preparing the daily summary should be carefully checked. Obviously, an error in giving change, in ringing up a sale, or neglecting to do so, will result in a cash shortage or overage. The daily summary provides spaces for such errors so that the proper entries can be made in your bookkeeping records. The last section of your daily summary, "Sales," records the total daily sales broken down into (1) cash sales and (2) charge sales.

As soon as possible after the daily summary has been completed, all cash for deposit should be taken to the bank. A duplicate deposit slip, stamped by the bank, should be kept with the daily summary as evidence that the deposit was made.

B. Petty Cash and Charge Funds

The record of, daily, sales and cash. Receipts which we have just described. is designed. on the assumption that a petty cash fund and a change cash fund, or a combination change and petty cash fund, are used. All businesses, small and large, have day-to-day expenses that are so small they do not warrant the drawing of a check. Good management practice calls for careful control of such expenses. The petty cash fund provides such control. It is a sum of money which is obtained by drawing a check to provide several days, a week's, or a month's need of cash for small purchases. The type of business will determine the amount of the petty cash fund.

Each time a payment is made from the petty cash, a slip should be made out. If an invoice or receipt is available, it should be attached to the petty- cash slip. The slips and the money ordinarily, but not necessarily, are kept separate from other currency in your cash till, drawer, or register. At all times, the total of unspent petty cash and petty cash slips should equal the fixed amount of the fund. When the total of the slips approaches the fixed amount of the petty cash fund, a check is drawn for the total amount of the slips. The money from this check is used to bring the fund back to its fixed amount.

In addition to a petty cash fund, some businesses that receive cash in over-the-counter transactions have a change fund. The amount needed for making change varies with the size and type of business, and, in some cases, with the days of the week. Control of the money in your change fund will be made-easier, however, if you set a fixed amount large enough to meet all the ordinary change-making needs of your business. Each day, when the day's receipts are balanced and prepared for a bank deposit, you will retain bills and coins totaling the fixed amount of the fund for use the following day. Since you had that amount on hand before you made the day's first sale, the entire amount of the day's receipts will still be available for your bank deposit.

In some cases, the petty cash fund is kept in a petty cash box or safe, apart from the change fund. However, the same fund can serve for both petty cash and change. For example, if you decide that you need $50 for making change and $25 for petty cash, one $75 fund can be used. Whenever, in balancing the day's operations, you see that the petty cash slips total more than $25, you can write a petty cash check for the amount of the slips.

C. Record of Cash Disbursement

To safeguard your cash, it is recommended that all receipts be deposited in a bank account and that all disbursements, except those made from the petty cash fund, are made by drawing a check on that account. Your bank account should be used exclusively for business transactions. If your business is typical, you will have to write checks for merchandise purchases, employee's salaries, rent, utilities, payroll taxes, petty cash, and various other expenses. Your check stubs will serve as a record of cash disbursements.

The checkbook stub should contain all the details of the disbursement including the date, payee, amount and purpose of the payment. In addition, a running balance of the amount you have in your bank account should be maintained by subtracting the amount of each check from the existing balance after the previous check was drawn. If the checks of your checkbook are prenumbered, it is important to mark plainly in the stub when a check is voided for one reason or another.

Each check should have some sort of written document to support it--an invoice, petty-cash voucher, payroll summary and so on. Supporting documents should be approved by you or someone you have authorized before a check is drawn. They should be marked paid and filed after the check is drawn.

Periodically, your bank will send you a statement of your account and return cancelled checks for which money has been withdrawn from your account. It is important that you reconcile your records with those of the bank. This means that the balances in your checkbook and on the bank statement should agree. Uncashed checks must be deducted from your checkbook balance and deposits not recorded on the bank statement must be added to its balance in order to get both balances to agree.

D . Accounts Receivable Records

If you extend credit to your customers, you must keep an accurate account of your credit sales not only in total as you have done on the daily summary but also by the amount that each individual customer owes you. Moreover, you must be systematic about billings and collections. This is important. It results in better relations with your charge customers and in fewer losses from bad debts.

The simplest method of handling accounts receivable--other than just keeping a file of sales-slip carbons--is to have an account sheet for each credit customer. Charge sales and payments on charge sales are posted to each customer sheet. Monthly billing to each of your charge customers should be made from their individual account sheets.

At least two or three times a year, your accounts receivable should be aged. You do this by posting each customer's account and his unpaid charges in columns according to age. These columns are labeled: not due; 1 to 30 days past due; 31 to 60 days past due; 61 to 90 days past due; etc. This analysis will indicate those customers who are not complying with your credit terms.

E . Property Records and Depreciation

In every type of business, it is necessary to purchase property and equipment from time to time. This property usually will last for several years, so it would be unrealistic to show the total amount of the purchase as an expense in any one year. Therefore, when this property is set up in the books as an asset, records must be kept to decrease its value over its life. This decrease is known as depreciation. I have mentioned this before during this talk. The amount of the decrease in value in one year, that is, the depreciation, is charged as an expense for the year.

I am talking about this expense, particularly, because no cash is paid out for it. It is a non-cash, not-out-of-pocket expense. You don't have to hand over actual money at the end of the month.

Records should be kept of this because, otherwise, there is a danger that this expense will be overlooked. Yet it is impossible to figure true profit or loss without considering it. When you deduct the depreciation expense from your firm's income, you reduce your tax liabilities. When you put this depreciation expense into a depreciation allowance account, you are keeping score on your "debt" to depreciation.

In a barber shop, to take a simple example, depreciation of its chairs, dryers, and clippers at the end of the year amounts to $136. You deduct this $136 from the shop's income, in this case, to pay the debt credited to your depreciation allowance account. Since this equipment has the same depreciation value each year, the depreciation allowance account at the end of 3 years will show that a total of $408 worth of equipment has been used up. The books of the barbershop therefore show an expense of $408 which actually has not been spent. It is in the business to replace the depreciated equipment. If replacement will not take place in the immediate future, the money can be used in inventory, or in some other way to generate more sales or profits.

How you handle this money depends on many things. You can set it aside at a low interest rate and have that much less operating money. Or you can put it to work in your business where it will help to keep your finances healthy.

Remember, however, that you must be prepared financially when it is time to buy replacement equipment. A depreciation allowance account on your books can help to keep you aware of this. It helps you keep score on how much depreciation or replacement money you are using in your business.

Keeping score with a depreciation allowance account helps you to know when you need to convert some of your assets into replacement cash. If, for example, you know on January 1 that Your delivery truck will be totally depreciated by June 30, you can review the situation objectively. You can decide whether you ought to use the truck longer or replace it. If you decide to replace it, then you can plan to accumulate the cash, and time the purchase in order to make the best deal.

F. Schedule of Insurance Coverage

The schedule of insurance coverage is prepared to indicate the type of coverage and the amount presently in force. This schedule should list all the insurance carried by your business--fire and extended coverage, theft, liability, life, business interruption and so forth.

This schedule should be prepared to present the following: name of insurance company, annual premium, expiration date, type of coverage, amount of coverage, asset insured, and estimated current value of asset insured.

An analysis of this schedule should indicate the adequacy of insurance coverage. A review of this schedule with your insurance agent is suggested.

V. CONCLUSION

During the brief time allotted to this subject of the basic fundamentals of bookkeeping, we have just scratched its surface. What we have tried to do is to inform you, as small-business managers, of the importance of good records. We have described the components of the important records that you must have if you are going to manage your business efficiently and profitably. In addition, we have brought to your attention some of the subsidiary records that will aid you in managing your business.

There are other records such as breakeven charts, budgets, cost accounting systems, to mention a few, which can also benefit the progressive manager. However, we do not have the time even to give you the highlights of those management tools. Your accountant can assist you in learning to understand and use them. Moreover, he can help you to develop and use the records we have discussed. For further information about them, you also can read the publications of the Small Business Administration, some of which are available to you free of charge.

By reading and using the accounting advice available to you, you can make sure that you have the right records to improve your managing skill and thereby increase your profits.

www.ingramcontent.com/pod-product-compliance
Lightning Source LLC
Chambersburg PA
CBHW082148300426
44117CB00016B/2659